Raising Peaceable Powerful Children

Barbara Hill Steinau

Writers Club Press
San Jose New York Lincoln Shanghai

Raising Peaceable Powerful Children

Published by Writers Club Press
an imprint of iUniverse.com, Inc.

For information address:
iUniverse.com, Inc.
5220 S 16th, Ste. 200
Lincoln, NE 68512
www.iuniverse.com

ISBN: 0-595-09809-6

Printed in the United States of America

for Mort
co-worker for justice
co-parent of our perky and active children
and partner extraordinaire

Contents

Foreword

About twenty-five years ago I began a student teaching experience that would change my life. Though hell-bent on becoming an elementary school teacher, I accepted a last-minute placement at the Gesell Institute Nursery School in New Haven, consoling myself that I would be free of doing lesson plans for a semester, and would get to play all morning with cute little kids. Barbara Hill Steinau, then director of the school, quickly but gently dispelled that notion.

What I learned during that semester (and over the next three years as a teacher at Gesell) gave me the rock-hard foundation needed to become an early childhood educator and an advocate for children. Barbara is the mason of that strong foundation.

Many teachers and parents speak of a special person who profoundly affected the course of their professional and parenting lives, someone who, early on, helped to shape their views, a mentor who guided their development as a raiser of young people.

What is it that makes their influence so profound? Passion! Barbara's exuberance and intelligence were contagious; she was so hungry to learn more about what she already knew so much about that I was bowled over. No source was irrelevant to Barbara, and it was the young people from whom she learned the most.

Mentors are respectful of the development process. They are keen observers who instinctively know when you're open to new information. Many have the crafty ability to guide a discussion your way, and you feel, euphorically, that the insight was your own. Barbara is a fisher, dropping the line and waiting for a bite. I am inspired by her, and know that I can reach beyond my grasp.

Barbara has been such a mentor for many. We came to appreciate how young people learn by watching Barbara watch children. It is both a science and an art. She is expert at helping parents who are angry or heartbroken. They come to trust her and can accept her support remarkably quickly.

In 1980 the Steinau School for Young Children was founded by a few of the parents and teachers whose lives Barbara Hill Steinau had touched. *"Raising Peaceable Powerful Children"* is the culmination of fifty years of experience and insight into what helps young children become capable and caring adults.

Denise DuClos
Director, Steinau School for Young Children

Preface & Acknowledgments

It isn't possible for me to acknowledge and thank, individually, each of the many people who've made this book possible. Heading the list are the young people—thousands of them, ages two to five—whom I've taught and nurtured. The opportunity to spend time with them and learn from them has been an enormous gift. Young people are ingenious, open to wonder, eager to learn. They have inspired me to look at life and teaching with freshness, and as a life-long journey of exploration and discovery. I have tried to communicate this understanding of children's ways and culture to scores of young teachers and to you, now, in this book.

As I did from the children, so have I learned from the teachers, many of whom were first-time teachers. New teachers, luckily, don't see the job of working with children as a rote combination of passing on information, instilling discipline, and getting them ready for the next grade, an all-too-common goal of nursery schools and preschools, not to mention kindergartens, elementary and high schools, and colleges. They are able to deal with *this* level of the student's life, *this* day, *this* second of stress, joy, disappointment, anger, openness.

Special teachers who've been of substantial help to me, in life and in the preparation of the book, are Judy Buzzell, Merle Thompson, Joan Stone, and Denise DuClos (who became the director of the Steinau School for Young Children after the closing of the Gesell Institute Nursery School in 1980). Each of these four gifted women became head teachers during my seventeen years at Gesell. Jan Piscitelli (a head teacher at Gesell who went with me to the Charlie Mills Preschool, which

I started at the Connecticut Hospice in Branford) and Rose Denny were important in my continuing education as a teacher and director.

An equally valuable contributor to my large pre-book notebook was Randy Griffin, an author and chef, in charge of the Hospice kitchen and dining room. During many walks and talks we discussed everything about young children, Randy frequently tape-recording our conversations. She later gave me typed transcriptions, which have been of tremendous help.

I give large and special thanks to my daughter Mardi, my editor, typist, re-typist, proofreader and book shepherd, whose creativity and zest for the material have augmented the book handsomely, and whose determination and diligence have kept the book alive (and I thank her partner Nancy for her considerable support of Mardi): my daughter Joan, an author of several books, a parent and a starter of schools, whose frequent ideas have bolstered me and educated me about book-writing; and my son Pete, a parent and unusually clear thinker who has given me strong moral support with his enduring faith in me.

I thank Scott Edelstein for his reading and comments about publication, John Murray for invaluable computer wizardry, and Patty Holman and Eleanor Strickland for typing, scanning, proofing and figuring out computer things. I thank *innumerable* others for reading, criticizing, supporting and cheering me and the book. My thanks are heartfelt.

I thank my parents, Zip and Ralph, for getting my philosophy started.

Lastly, and always, I thank my husband and partner Mort, for support too far-reaching and amazing to describe.

Introduction

I want to tell you about my system of teaching, gradually evolving over a thirty-five year period. It deals with children in a thoughtful, compassionate manner. I am aware of children's rights, of their innate abilities, of their capacity to grow if unstifled. This approach transfers power to the children rather than to the adult. It enables children to learn, rather than teaching them. It recognizes the energy that is present in children to learn. It provides the setting and the ambiance, and then steps out of the way. It respects children, which encourages them to respect themselves. Children learn to become less dependent on adults, and thus settle issues between themselves. They become peacemakers.

My parents were free thinkers. They questioned, they wondered, they voted for third-party candidates. I remember having to sit in the back of the school bus because I was wearing an Al Smith button, and everyone else was for Hoover. I had the model before me of questioning, of acting on one's convictions, whether or not they were the popular thought. My mother and uncle planned to vote for the two mainstream candidates (one for each) but then decided to cancel out each other's votes by voting for Wallace, the third-party candidate. They felt that third parties should have a chance, and devised this method of implementing their wishes without taking anything away from their candidates of choice.

I have always been proud of knowing that my father would have gone to jail rather than to fight in World War I. I'm glad to know that he would have acted on his convictions with such strength. He became a missionary and went to teach in Aintab, Turkey, and did not have a chance to test his convictions, but I believe he would have done what was necessary to uphold it. I loved hearing the stories of the life he and my mother led in Turkey for two years. My mother was not employed as a teacher, but saw that the local women desperately needed work. She helped them start a lace factory, where they pooled their resources and broke down some of the isolation that defined their lives. She was a model to me just as much as my father was. I saw them see situations, decide what needed to be done, and do it.

My parents stood outside the prison where Sacco and Vanzetti were executed. They were part of a demonstration standing up for the rights of the two men, believing that they had been framed. They protested the executions.

I attended several progressive schools in my early years. Lincoln School in New York City and the Marietta Johnson School in Alabama both furthered my thinking. In each of these, children were taught and encouraged to think for themselves. Education was viewed as a process. It is exciting to learn when one is pressed to figure things out. I was pushed to take chances and no one laughed at failure. I am convinced that in these settings I became a free thinker.

Later I attended Black Mountain College, an experimental college in North Carolina. At Black Mountain there were no grades, no outside judgments. It was assumed that one wanted to learn, to think, to argue, and to try out different points of view. There were not traditional year-by-year standings, but rather a junior and senior division, and students progressed from one to the other to graduation at their own rates. I remember two of the questions I had to answer in order to move from the junior to senior division: "How do you know the sky is blue?" and "How do you know the Philippine Islands exist?" Rote thinking was not at the heart of such a place. These questions look for creativity and daring.

It was my children who actually moved me into the early-childhood field. In New Jersey we wanted our eldest child to attend a Quaker School, but could not afford the tuition. I was offered the chance to become an assistant teacher in the nursery program in exchange for her fee. I seized the opportunity. Our second child accompanied me to this class, which was difficult for him and for me. I expected him to be the best-behaved child in the room, or ignored him, or was over-conscious of him. In later years, as director of early-childhood centers, I have often remembered this experience, and have been reluctant to hire teachers when their own children would have attended their classes. Though one occasion proved workable for both child and mother, it was more often the case that both felt burdened. Children and their adult caregivers need the opportunity to deal with others in the classroom, without the intrusion of the delicate parental relationship.

We moved to Connecticut. Our third child had been ready to enter kindergarten in New Jersey. At that time Connecticut had no public kindergartens. I opened a school primarily so that she would not be disappointed. It fascinates me that our older daughter did the same thing, many years later, when she moved to Martha's Vineyard and found no school there for her young daughter. The school she established, Island Children's School, exists to this day.

My concern for my own children's well-being led me to enter a field which has become my life work. My leadership qualities made it possible for me to be the director, as well as teacher, in the schools I joined or started. I was the one able to set the tone of the school, the one who could train teachers who would at least partially reflect my views of what was appropriate for the education of young children. At the time I entered the field, large numbers of parents and teachers held attitudes of which I disapproved. I regret to say that I still find that to be generally true.

Although a director most of my life, I've been fortunate to be a teacher as well. Only once, for a year, did I find myself directing and administering without teaching. I quickly arranged things so that this would never happen again. I missed very much the actual teaching of young people, and missed being out on the floor with other teachers. My modeling for them is one of the keystones to my approach. We try out different angles to a given situation with a particular child, and discuss them with each other. I don't find theoretical solutions as valid as those that emerge from hands-on experience.

I've been fortunate to have had such opportunities to teach and develop. I've been able to open new programs. I began a class for two-year-olds and their parents, before so many adults found themselves forced to join the labor force. Parents made the commitment to stay the two hours each day in order to learn more about their children, and to build some experience with young children in general. They observed the two teachers working with their child and other children; they observed their child's responses to the teachers and to other children; they had a chance to be teachers themselves and to try out new approaches. Each day the parents also met together briefly to mull over some of the things that had happened that day.

I've known two child therapists whose practices were unusual, and I have adopted some of them. One practiced hug therapy. He believed that most of us suffer from a lack of hugging, and he asked parents to hug their children during sessions. It didn't matter whether or not the child appeared to like it. The important thing was for the parent to keep on hugging regardless of the protestations of the child. The child might try to slip out of the hug, and the parent was to hang on. The child might say, "Stop it. I don't want you to hug me," but the parent was to keep hugging. Sometimes the child laughed while protesting. Laughing is a form of discharging feelings. We're all familiar with the nervous laughter of adults when nothing is funny. The more the child laughs, the more she is letting off pent-up feelings. She may cry, and crying drains off pain, anger, and sadness. The parent keeps hugging, and saying, in effect, "I'm right here for you. You may have felt that sometimes I wasn't. Now I am, and you can count on it."

I still have problems with an insistence on holding when a person doesn't want to be held. However, there is something about this approach that interested me extremely. None of us gets all of the reassurance we need. None of us has gotten all the physical affection we have needed over the years. In my schools I had always hugged children often, whether they seemed to particularly enjoy it or not. Then I began to realize that there were some who almost wriggled out of my arms. It occurred to me that these might be the children who most lacked hugging; for some reason it was difficult for them to accept it. I eventually found that, when I was persistent, they usually melted in my arms. Sometimes this took days, because their resistance was strong. I believe that such children had been let down at some point in their lives, and could no longer count on someone close to them. They had developed protective coloring: "I don't care." My theory, that we need all the physical affection and reassurance of love that we can get, seemed to have been affirmed.

Then, some years ago, I invented what I call a hugging trap. I would sit on the floor with arms wide open, announcing that I was a hugging trap. Children would run past me, getting near, and yet trying not to get close enough for me to envelop them. It was interesting to discern the patterns different children began to evidence. Some would practically fall into the trap. Others would skirt the trap, getting closer and closer, until they were captured and hugged. A few would stay far enough away that it took quite a bit of maneuvering on my part to eventually catch and hug them. When I finally did, they giggled and giggled. I believe they were releasing feelings which they needed to release. It was curious that those children who asked most to play the hugging trap were the ones who made it the most difficult for me to catch them. Children would usually want to play this game much longer than I did. I would tire while they were eager to continue. I think these children were doing something they were afraid of, in order to conquer fear, and something they also very much wanted. I'm saddened to realize that any child is afraid of hugs.

Another therapist told me that he routinely copies the posture of young patients, in order to help them feel more comfortable in his office. He is not dramatic or mocking about it, but simply assumes the same general position as the child. If a child is sitting crosslegged, he crosses his legs. If a child puts a hand up to her face, so does he. His face displays nothing but warmth, and the child does not feel embarrassed. He firmly believes that he should make the patient as comfortable as he can.

I thought I would do something similar. I discovered that I could use this approach often, particularly with children visiting the school for the first time. When a new child visits, I usually take her to the sand table. Sand is a non-threatening material with which there is no possibility of failure. I get down on my knees, to be at the child's level, and start pouring sand from one container to another. I don't speak much to the child; I may describe what I'm doing. "I'm pouring sand through and watching it make a pile." Children usually become easily involved in watching me work. I move some similar implements near the child, who is across the table from me. I may or may not tell the child they are for her. I assess how comfortable the child is becoming. If she seems slow to acclimate herself to the surroundings and to my company, I'll say nothing, and merely indicate that they are for her use. Eventually she picks up the implements and begins to move sand. Then I switch to copying her behavior. If she picks up a funnel, so do I. If she places it upside down in the sand, so do I. The amount of talking I do continues to depend on my sense of her comfort, since I feel that talking can be intrusive.

I don't intrude on the child. I don't request that she do something, which she is likely to refuse from initial discomfort or perform for my approval. I demonstrate some of the ways that sand can be played with. As soon as she feels safe enough to play, I mirror her movements. She feels a sense of power; she is leading me. She probably felt nervous and at least partially powerless as she entered this strange building. My goal is to give back some of her power as soon as I can. Mirroring her movements has proven remarkably effective.

A benefit of this approach is that it gives me an excellent chance to study the child. I can get a sense of her, and make an assessment as to how I think she would fit into the group. Children often ask me for one of my implements at the sand table. I usually refuse to share it, saying that I am using it now, and that I will gladly relinquish it soon. One of the most difficult aspects for a young child in a social situation is the sharing of equipment. I want her to learn, right away, that not everything is available to her instantly. Since another child might not respond to her request in as friendly a fashion as I do, I want her to see in a warm and natural way that she won't necessarily be able to have everything she wants when she wants it. I hear, understand and respect her request for the tool, and make it clear that desires are important; they simply can't always be granted immediately. I may say, "I can tell how much you want to use this big spoon with holes in it. Thank you for telling me. When I am through I will be happy to give it to you." I want her to hear this message, and I want her to hear it first from me.

What can parents and caregivers take from the applications of the two therapies I've discussed? Parents need to be aware of the importance of physical affection. Many parents do lots of hugging and kissing. Others do not, either because they are not demonstrative people or because they get signals from their children which say they don't want it. Some parents tell me that from the first few days of a child's life she stiffens and cries when being hugged. They have, not surprisingly, kept hands off much of the time since. It's to these parents that I speak. I urge you to try some of what I have mentioned above. I believe that you will discover that your child *will* protest, will at some point allow your hugs, and will finally enjoy and request physical contact. I don't know what makes the defenses of some young children so strong. I believe that it is our job to break through them. Are there times when you put up defenses which you hope will be broken? When I attend cocktail parties or large social gatherings, I'm the best cracker-passer in attendance because I'm afraid of meeting new people. I'm afraid they won't want to talk to me, so I make myself very busy. I'm hoping that someone will approach me and make it easy for me to get into conversation, although my body language gives the lie to this.

Fortunately, my ruse often works, and people pull me into conversation. You may be able to think of situations where you erect defenses you hope will be ineffective. If so, you may have strong sympathy for your child.

Mirroring a child's behavior is often an effective and warm, easy way for a parent to play with her/his child. Children like it when an adult allows them to take the lead. A parent can easily do this when playing. Let the child supply the ideas, do the planning, make the first move. This kind of play will prove popular with most children. It shouldn't replace the kind of parent/child activity wherein the child is engaged in grown-up work along with her parent, as in carpentry and cooking. Both kinds of parent/child interactions are important, those when the child leads and those when the parent leads. Both are ways to build a sense of self-worth and competence, and both convey a level of acceptance of the child. Many children are given the opportunity to share grown-up work, but fewer are given the chance to lead their parents. They get a lovely message. "My mom thinks I have good ideas; she'll do what I do. I must be a capable person; I must be fun to be with."

I wrote this book because I have seen many parents raising peaceable, powerful children. Such young people impress me. I can imagine what effective and delightful adults they will become. I also believe, however, that many other parents and teachers are struggling mightily to nurture young people, and are so overwhelmed with difficulties they often do not know what to do. It's hard to treat children in ways that raise and protect their self-esteem; it's equally difficult to teach effective methods of solving problems without fighting. I am convinced that all parents and teachers want to help bring forth peaceable, powerful young people.

We're not always fortunate enough to have mentors, or role-models, to help and lead us. Colleagues can be a vital source of support. I've also depended on reading, and intend this book as a friend to those of you seeking directness, open-mindedness, and respect in your care-giving.

In thirty-five years of working with young children, one of my primary goals has been to help them learn to negotiate, and to solve problems in peaceful ways. I don't think fighting is effective. I have taught teachers to spend a great deal of time listening to struggles between four-year-olds, and then to restate what they hear. "Emily, you're saying that Yusuf had this truck first. Tell Yusuf what you just told me." "Yusuf, you are saying that you want that truck. Let Emily know that." When children have strong feelings about something, it is hard for them to hear another point of view (as is often the case with adults). When statements are reflected back through a teacher, it is often easier for children to hear each other, because adults provide safety. We help with this process over and over again, and each time the child picks up a little bit of awareness about how to solve problems.

When children have moved on to other schools, we have often heard from their new teachers that their ability to work out interpersonal problems was unusually good. Such confirmation is the reward we need to help us keep up the time-consuming and repetitious work of teaching children how to listen to each other and to compromise.

The second aspect of child-rearing on which we focus is self-esteem. We believe that high self-esteem is an enormous key to living successfully and pleasurably. We enhance self-esteem in young children by taking them seriously, and by affirming them as often as possible. When we look at a painting a child is making, we describe what we see. "I see that you have a long yellow streak across the top, and now you're putting in lots of green dots along the side." We never say, "What a pretty picture." I don't believe in making such a value judgment, because I don't want to encourage children to depend on my assessment of the worth of the picture or the child. Describing the work indicates interest, and that we appreciate the effort put into the work. We might add, "I can see how hard you are working on that painting. You're stopping and thinking about how to do each part." We are not praising but appreciating.

When a child arrives in the morning we greet her. "Hello, I'm glad to see you." Throughout the day we give messages that show we enjoy her just for being. We like them because they are themselves. When children truly believe this, they can experiment, make mistakes, and create, because they know that their worth is not affected by performance.

Peaceable, powerful children will become peaceable, powerful adults. I believe it takes people who feel good about themselves to turn the world around. They are the people who can visualize world peace.

I hope that this book can provide a lifeline to teachers and parents working to raise children in our materialistic, violent and competitive society. My beliefs acknowledge the stresses on modern parents and teachers, and the loneliness felt by many adults who relate to children. I support child-raisers and honor your work, and I hope to gently lead you to more and effective ways to lead.

I write from a long history of parenting and teaching. I've been director and teacher at two well-known institutions for thirty-five years, and have trained hundreds of teachers to be accepting, thoughtful, feeling and effective guides of young children, and to become child advocates rather than child controllers. Observing, listening and reading during my long and happy years with preschool children, I realized that I was developing new ideas and approaches that were a blend of my experiences and the experiences of others. I saw what usually helped children bloom.

When I have the opportunity to teach teachers, which I enjoy as much as I do teaching young children, I find they are generally able to see the sense in what I am pointing out, and are eager to grow into more adept facilitators of young children's education. I have worked under few true mentors, but have learned a phenomenal amount through my membership to the magazine *Young Children* for thirty-five years. This is the publication of the NAEYC (National Association for the Education of Young Children). It has been one of my important teachers.

Teachers I've trained have also been my teachers. Having a teacher question what I am teaching is one of my favorite ways to learn. Having to defend and explain solidifies my thinking and allows me to change my thinking. Interchange with others has been a key element of my professional growth. I feel deeply sorry for the many teachers who have little of this. I'm sure that it greatly limits their development. Mirrors help us see what we are doing and how we are doing it. One of the wonderful aspects of teaching young children has been the fact that there are always several teachers working together with one class. There's a greater opportunity to see children with more clarity when teachers bounce ideas and observations off each other.

As a member of and writer for the NAEYC, I often lecture to groups of teachers. I am active in encouraging other teachers and parents to make the best possible environment for vibrant growth to thrive. As mother of three children and grandmother of three children, I've had an opportunity to look at situations from a parent's side, as well. As a teacher, it's easy to become impatient with parents, forgetting that parents do the best they can. With help, parents gladly make changes when they can see that they are in the best interests of their children.

Countless books have been written about parenting. Their number indicates how much parents want to learn and grow, and to be appreciated for what they already do. *Raising Peaceable Powerful Children* does not offer techniques as much as it offers a particular way of looking at and appreciating children. Confident parents can make up their own techniques and develop their own methodology. I do include many anecdotes and examples, however, which illustrate my philosophy and values.

My developing values and standards have influenced me as a person and as a parent and teacher. I have gained a sense of personal integrity, a sense of who I am and what I believe, and responsibility to act on those beliefs.

It is important to me that I interrupt injustices to myself or to another. I tell people how their actions and words affect me. Sometimes I share these experiences later with others, telling them what I said and what the reaction was like. In this way I magnify the results of my actions. Someone may say to me, "My, you don't look seventy-nine," thinking that they're paying me a compliment. I used to say, "Thank you." I no longer accept such remarks as compliments, but reply, "Well, this is the way one seventy-nine-year-old looks." When people use racial stereotypes in my hearing, I let it be known that they make me very uncomfortable, trying to emphasize the contents of the remarks, not a failure by the speaker.

I combat racism, sexism, fear of homosexuality, adultism, anti-Semitism, ableism. The three most commonly affecting young children are sexism, racism and adultism. My definition of adultism is the use of power over children in unfair, sneaky and manipulative ways.

I am distressed at the effect of the media on young children and their parents. Children are often socialized early in their lives to prefer the company of their own gender, to play with the equipment that manufacturers have determined to be appropriate for their gender and to engage in the kinds of play such equipment suggests. As a teacher of young children I do all in my power to give both genders ample opportunity to escape strictures placed on them by society, and reinforce the stretching and breaking of stereotypes.

I act often, as a teacher and as a member of society, on my concern that people and nations deal with each other in a peaceful fashion. I teach negotiation to those with whom I come in contact, and encourage young children to learn communication tools. Children can be taught to use words rather than fists. Worldwide use of negotiation can prevent wars. The media, which sponsors and promotes violence to a distressing degree, is an area with which I am concerned.

I believe that competition is one of the factors which encourages aggression between people, including children. I teach and play cooperative games, wherein we can value each other as unique while cooperating with each other as a group. Cooperation brings out invention and joy in all of us, and does not depend on adult approval.

I think that praise is generally non-productive as a teaching tool if one's goal is to help children build confidence in their own abilities. Praise is an extrinsic motivator. We want children to reward themselves internally, with pleasure, friendship, self-esteem and orderly growth. There is a subtle difference between praise and affirmation. Praise is judgmental, rating people or projects against external standards. Affirmation is a way of letting people know that we appreciate them as human beings, and are interested and excited by what they are doing.

I de-emphasize materialism. When children are given interesting raw materials like blocks, sand, water and paint, they develop their own creative abilities. We can wean young people from their dependence on commercial toys which stultify ingenuity. Adults can reinforce creativity. "The sand was flat a minute ago and you've made lots of tiny hills in it."

I believe that order encourages effective work and growth. The more shelves there are for toys, the more order is possible. Picture-signs encourage returning things to their place. Children respond well to order, and to knowing the approximate shape of their day. They can predict the next activity and savor the day's order.

I wrote this book to help grown-ups learn to deal straightforwardly and simply with their children. I'm honest. When a child is having difficulty in letting her parent leave her at school, I might say, "It's really hard for you to let your mom leave. You want her to stay with you. It's all right if you cry when she leaves. I'll stay with you until you feel better." The child knows that I, as the teacher, know what a difficult time she is having. She knows that it's all right to show how she feels, and she knows that I believe that the problem is important. Her dealing with this separation, I believe, is far more important right now than learning to color inside lines or reciting the alphabet. She will learn those things when she is ready.

Children often watch news on television, and what makes news is often frightening and violent. I'm glad when parents discuss the news with their children if they *do* allow them to watch it, and perhaps even more delighted when young children aren't allowed to watch the news. Children usually imagine the worst, and need a slow, careful context to be built around harsh concepts like murder and starvation.

My most recent job was director for ten years at the Charlie Mills Preschool at the Connecticut Hospice in Branford, Connecticut. This is the first free-standing hospice in the country, modeled on St. Christopher's in London. At first the school was primarily filled with children of hospice staff; many other local parents were initially reluctant to send their children to a school in a building where people were dying. Fortunately there were a number of parents who saw the possibilities for education in such a setting. They believed that it was important for children to know about death and sickness in real-life situations with people whom they knew only casually. They subscribed to my theory that children can be inoculated by small doses of experience. We believe that young people are better able to cope with the death of intimates if they have had other exposures to death. Concomitant with such exposure is the opportunity to discuss death. When a family member dies, the family is usually too grief-stricken to give a child the attention she requires, and may be unable or unwilling, at such a time, to answer simply and directly the child's questions and reactions. We felt lucky to nurture a school in such a setting.

The school was in its own separate wing, so our contact with patients was minimal. On those occasions when we made arrangements to visit a patient, such visits were always welcomed. We found out later from nurses that the patients were usually more direct in talking about their illnesses with the children than they were with their families. They enjoyed the simple, open questions of three-and four-year-olds. Such visits also put a human and personal face on dying; young children are not yet able to understand death as a concept, or in the abstract.

Raising children is a time-consuming job. Parents need to give a lot of themselves to the child. It takes a great deal of energy. If a parent gets up, goes over to a child, puts a hand on a shoulder and says, "I know it's hard to stop working with those blocks. Now it's time to wash for supper, but maybe you'll have a chance to build a little more after supper," the child is likely to respond more positively than to a brusque call to supper. I hope parents can be convinced that extra effort such as this is worth it. It is a matter of taking the long view. If a child doesn't respond until the third time she is called, the parent has used up a lot of nervous energy, and has become irritated, and when the child does finally respond, there is likely to be tension because of her delaying tactics.

The same principle applies in teaching children to share. If two children are fighting over a toy and a parent calls out, "Remember to share!" the child is not learning anything except that sharing means giving up what she wants. A parent, recognizing that a learning situation is at hand, can respond to a squabble by approaching the two with "It sounds as though you have a problem, two children and one doll." The children might respond by each claiming a right to the toy, and the parent's job is to stay out of refereeing, to bounce things back to the children. "I wonder how you are going to work it out?" implies that they have the power to do so. When a child suggests a solution, the parent can say, "You are really working on solving this problem." A parent can feel good about spending this kind of time in teaching critical life skills, and can also assume that the next fight might be speedier and less difficult.

I think that none of us counted on having to spend that kind of time with our children, that our job was to fix supper, call them to it and they would come; or that by calling out "Remember to share!" we would cause them to become generous people. What we didn't know was that we would have to be their teachers.

I remember a book from many years ago called *Where Did You Go? Out. What Did You Do? Nothing.* The title makes me remember a powerful message: we all need time to do nothing. Whenever a parent applies to my school, and early in the conversation says that her or his child is bored, I suspect that this is a child whose life has been over-programmed, one who has not had an opportunity to make choices to explore, and one who hasn't had a chance to simply hang out.

In this decade, and perhaps for the last several, I believe that middle-class Americans feel that they must schedule their children's days full of educational activities. One of the aspects of children's lives that needs attention is a major opportunity of childhood: to do nothing, and to have the leisure to figure out for themselves what they are going to do. Many teenagers have difficulty in using free time productively because they had little previous opportunity to plan their own time.

In what profession other than parenthood would we give people unlimited responsibility with no training? No wonder that a lot of grown-up ex-children have little self-discipline, no love for their work, low self-esteem, and difficulty in feeling concern and empathy for others. They've been raised by parents who had no training for the job.

Raising children wasn't always so difficult. Extended families provided more models for parents and more hands-on help in child-rearing. The world was also a little smaller, providing fewer occupations and less distraction. Family businesses or trades sometimes offered the footprints of parents, that children might follow.

Today parents raising children are much more on their own. Their own parents are often far away. Most families do not have the luxury of one member staying at home to raise children. Life is hurried. Parents generally do the work of raising children the way their own parents did, since that is the chief model available. Some parents want to do things differently. They might say, "My parents were too strict with me. I'm not going to be that way with my children." Yet it's very hard to do it differently, and parents feel conflict, doing what they do not want to do since they know no other way.

Some have suggested that there be a compulsory course in child-rearing and homemaking. If males and females were required to take such a course we might become a better-functioning society. They would become clearer about whether or not they wanted to be parents; if they did, they would become clearer about how they really want to parent; they would have a clearer sense of themselves; they might be freer to feel, and to show compassion.

The effects of entrusting sensitive beings to untutored parents cannot be overstated. Children are vastly impressionable, and eager to learn what is happening around and to them. We are coming to realize that child abusers are usually people who were abused as children. What a striking example of how we may well become the kind of people our parents were. We need to look for and find opportunities and models that will help us break the cycle of repeating whatever ways our parents raised us that were ineffective.

Since there are not yet many classes in parenting, how can parents get help now? Some form support groups. As a young parent I found such a group helpful. It was a place to check out my instincts and find out from other parents their views on bedtimes, eating, toilet training. We shared triumphs and failures, and I didn't have to pretend I was a perfect parent. It was useful to discover that I wasn't the only one in despair over my inability to get my four-year-old to sleep. We comforted each other.

Some parents find support and guidance through reading. The tricky part, of course, is to find books that are truly supportive. Don't read books that make you feel like a terrible parent.

In two- or multiple-parent families, each adult can be of tremendous use and support to the other; they can observe and comment in helpful ways on each other's parenting. When we are enmeshed in sticky situations, it can be almost impossible to see what is happening. A sympathetic observer may be able to help us disentangle ourselves. When my daughter was four, she came home from nursery school with a phrase that drove me crazy. Everything was "Stinkin' spootyatty!" She learned immediately, of course, that I didn't like it. I was so caught up in my frustration that I needed her father's gentle observations, and was able to stop showing my reaction. She dropped the phrase quickly.

As the state of economic disarray worsens in this and many other countries, most families require more money than was provided by the old, one-income model family. Family groupings, too, are changing definition, and TV and the press are noticing that people who care for children may be single adults, or same-sex partners, or child-care cooperatives, or intergenerational related adults. No matter the contours of the family, one income rarely suffices any more. The adult or adults likely face difficulties in arranging for child care. Mornings are rushed, with no breakfast or a hurried one, and pressure may be brought to bear on children. In these circumstances, it is not easy to go off to school and learn what they must, or to relax and enjoy their own lives.

If a child is sick, the caregivers worry throughout the day about whether the child is all right. "Am I a bad parent because I put my work first? Will the back-up baby-sitter be able to pick her up? Is my work suffering from all this worry?"

It's a balancing act. It's important to make time for yourself, but it can be very hard. A rushed parent finds it difficult to give genuine and effective care to anyone.

Teachers and day-care workers are often critical of parents, based on what they observe at drop-off and pick-up time. I found that frequently this was due to inadequate communication. I like to encourage parents to stay in touch with me, and let me know what major things are happening at home. Though I believe in children's privacy at many levels, I find it appropriate that teachers and parents share information and insights about their children, supporting each others' efforts in lending strength and intelligence to the struggles of children.

As I was walking one day on a trail through the Cape Cod woods, I rounded a curve and saw a spectacular marsh, hummocks of grass pushing up through the water as far as I could see. I saw others enjoying the sight. A young woman was sitting with an easel in her lap, a palette in her hand, and a brush poised. I watched her for a moment, and then realized there was another artist present. Near her was a boy about four years old. In his lap he held a large pad of paper, and next to him was a basket of crayons. He too was studying the marsh, and drawing what he saw. I was intrigued, and stood quietly watching the pair of artists. There was little conversation; each was engaged by the task. It was clear that each respected the work and the space of the other by not intruding upon it.

I've thought often of this mother and of the way she was able to do her work without the intrusion of her child. She included him by treating him seriously as a fellow artist. I imagine that they may have talked about their own work to each other at the conclusion of their time at the marsh. I imagine that neither criticized the other's work. I assume that each appreciated the efforts of the other. I can imagine the boy saying to his mother, "Gee, Mom, you can really paint so I can still see the marsh." I picture the mother talking to him. "I like to see how you study the marsh carefully before you use the crayons." Each is affirming the other.

I like to think of this boy as he grows up. He may become an artist like his mother or not, but he will certainly grow up feeling good about himself. He will have a sense of himself as a competent human being. He will not have the need to irritate to gain the attention of others; he gets plenty of attention legitimately. He and his mother have a warm and supportive relationship. She rarely needs to say 'no' to him; she finds ways of affirming him so that she reinforces the behavior she thinks is healthy. I think he will be well-liked by his peers and comfortable with adults. His basic need for approval has been well met.

Part One

Stereotypes And Ism's

The male pronoun, "he," is characteristically used when the gender of a person is not known, or not specified. I consider this sexism, and have considered how to counteract such oppression of females. I've thought of various options: 'she\he;' 's/he;' 'co' (a neuter noun used, among other places, at Twin Oaks, an intentional community in Virginia); 'she' when referring to a child; and alternating 'she' and 'he," either every other time or at random. None of the above possibilities is really an effective solution at this particular moment in history, but I strongly believe it's vital for us to try to change our language in order to help change the world's thinking. I've chosen, therefore, to use 'she' when speaking of a child of unknown or unspecified gender, and to use 'he' and 'she' at all other times. I expect that my choice will jar some readers' ears. I apologize if it interferes with thoughtful perusal of my writing. It's my hope that it stirs many readers to contemplate the use of sexist language, and think about how it helps perpetuate sexism in society.

I've been interested in discovering various authors' concerns about the issue of sexist language. I've found, though, that they generally end up by reverting to the traditional 'he.' I'm reassured when I find people aware of the problem, but discouraged at the apparent inability to take risks and break out of old patterns.

In working with young children, it's vital that we shake ourselves loose from stereotypical approaches. A stereotype is an oversimplified generalization about a particular group, one that usually carries overt or subtle derogatory implications. When choosing books, we notice how females are presented; how old people are characterized; how people of various races and ethnic origin are depicted. Too often females are shown as passive, African Americans as happy-go-lucky and servile, or pushy and violent, old people as bent and feeble. In order to avoid transmitting stereotypes to our child, we can look for and use only books which do not include them, or change the wording of the text. I often expurgate when reading aloud to young children. For instance, I cut out the word 'old' before 'woman' or 'man' when the age of the character is not pertinent to the story. I cut out some of the sweet, soft words describing young girls, and some of the tough, macho words describing boys. The story doesn't suffer; my listeners profit by their lessening of exposure to damaging stereotypes which support limiting and untrue ideas about groups of people. We get our ideas about others from hearing and watching those around us, by absorbing them from the media (books and television being the two prime affecters of young children). I often cross out words in books which I find offensive or inaccurate. When children ask me why I have written in a book, I tell them that the author had inaccurate information and I want to be sure not to tell them things that are not true.

The majority of books for young children still show males as more adventuresome, more active, more creative than females. In some instances, I change the wording so that the female makes some of the daring, exciting statements. In a few cases I have been able to change a boy to a girl by adding pigtails. When you find books for your young children, please take time to assess the stereotypes.

Children need to have models of the world as we wish them to see it. If we want them always to see girls with dolls and boys with trucks it is easy to find books showing these activities. If we want them to be aware of limitless possibilities for themselves, we can look for books to expand their horizons, not narrow them.

Look for books which show people of color in responsible jobs, as intelligent, thoughtful people. Check the illustrations. Are people of color shown as genuine individuals, or are they fat, happy, physically powerful, rhythmic, etc.? We need to watch for loaded words like lazy, backward, docile. Note the setting for people of color. Do they live in a ghetto? Is there a mixture of whites and people of color, or is each group shown separately with the introduction of one person of color in a servile role, such as maid? Children are often more influenced by society's attitudes than they are by their parents. I encourage non-racist, non-sexist books in order to guide young children in non-stereotypical thinking.

Look at the copyright date. Since the late sixties there has been a growing awareness of the importance of these issues. A recent copyright date will by no means insure any particular book's absence of prejudice, but it is more probable that it will reflect some of what I consider progress in awareness.

A children's librarian may be of help in this area. Most of the books for young children still present at least some stereotypes. It's not easy to find books I'm willing to read to young children. Some for which I settle are classics, in which I've done some revision and deletion. I think it's helpful for children to understand that books are written by people, and that those people are fallible, so I'm comfortable telling them that I didn't like the way the author wrote a certain part and have changed it. I always read the name of the author and the illustrator out loud. In this era, children actually see very few things being made, and don't really understand that things are made by people, or by people operating machines. They think that things are just there for them, for their pleasure. In order to give them a glimmer of this I talk much about authors and illustrators. I want them to know that people can make mistakes, in books as in life, and that we can disagree with their ideas.

Teachers, parents and other adults affect our children in many ways; they are aware of what we adults say and what we do. It's important for us to discuss stereotypes so that children will be aware of them and will not necessarily be limited by them. It is equally important for us to check our own behavior. Do we respond differently to girls and to boys?

Do we respond differently to children of color and to white children? Our own behavior is a model to our children. They see our reactions and copy them.

I recently visited a school where the teachers were unusually aware of stereotyping. These two teachers had been thoughtful in choosing books. They were conscious of racial stereotypes, and used very little discriminatory language. And yet I noticed they responded quite differently to the boys than to the girls. They encouraged the boys in vigorous activity much more than the girls. When there seemed to be an opening in an active game on the playground, they more often invited boys to join than girls. They almost exclusively encouraged same-gender play, not having considered reinforcing cross-gender play by commenting on what a good time Maria and Jose were having building sand castles together.

After the school day ended, I met with the two teachers to discuss my observations. I was able to tell them of many things I appreciated about their teaching. When I then commented on their reinforcement of gender-based play, they were surprised. They were not defensive, perhaps because I had been able to point out their abundant strong points as well. They immediately wanted to discuss ways they could overcome this weakness in their teaching. I felt refreshed to find teachers so open to change. We talked about ways in which they might encourage girls to be more physically active and traded ideas for fostering more girl\boy play.

When I next visited the school, I was delighted with their success in accomplishing our goals. There was very little division by gender throughout the day. Boys and girls joined in many types of play, both passive and assertive, both physical and creative. It excites me to see how readily children's behavior can change when the adults around them change. When we open ourselves to new ideas without being defensive and make conscious decisions to change our own behavior, our children thrive.

Choosing a Preschool or Daycare Center

The first step in choosing a center is probably an interview with the director. From her or him you should be able to acquire a sense of the philosophy of the school. Listen for the aspects of early childhood education that are important at the center. If the values stressed by the director match your values, plan to continue your investigation of the center by observing the teachers. An hour or so of observing the class your child would join will give you a perspective on the teaching styles.

How do the teachers and the children interact? Do teachers really listen to children, or are their answers perfunctory? Do they get down physically to the child's level so that their eyes meet easily? How do they act when a child is unhappy, hurt, or scared? Do they let the child know that they understand her feelings, and do they give her comfort? Do they dismiss the child's feelings as unimportant, and try to distract her from them? Are the teachers talking mostly to each other, or are they observing the children and responding to them as needed?

In an effective preschool, the teachers spend much of their time squatting, approximating the height of the young people. Because the teachers are carefully observing the children, they know when to move in to assist a child in solving a problem, and when to let the child struggle with the problem. The staff is well-trained in giving children freedom. The freedom to fail is one of the most precious gifts we can offer. We learn from our failures, perhaps more than from successes.

Another essential freedom is the ability of grown-ups and children to be honest with one another. Sensitive teachers believe that crying is useful for children when they are hurt or unhappy. Teachers can squarely acknowledge the feelings of children. "I know you are missing your dad. You wish he were here right now. I wish he were here, too, and I'll bet *he* wants to be here. I'm going to give you a hug and hold you while you are feeling so sad." This is not the time to urge the child into activities; her feelings are dignified by acceptance and attention. When the child has calmed down, the teacher can help her gradually join others in play.

What kind of voices do the teachers use? Are they sweet and syrupy; do they sound false or real? Do they sound as though they genuinely like children and are happy to be there with them? Do they treat the children with dignity, or talk down to them?

Do the teachers move around so that they are on hand for the action? Do they stay in one place, expecting the children to come to them? Are the teachers aware of the quiet children? Do they offer attention even when it is not actively sought?

Think of how you want your child cared for. If you were a teacher in her school, you would be noticing her needs, and figuring out how to be useful to and supportive of her. You would probably relish working together cooperatively with the other teachers. You would probably check in with them about decisions you made throughout the day. Watch the teaching in this center, pick a child and follow her progress for an hour. What do you feel about the environment of that particular child?

Take a look at the daily schedule of the center. Does the school follow regular routines, so that children can predict what will happen next? Young children need to have a sense of the day's flow. With the security of order, they can also be flexible. The schedule should be flexible, too, and allow for unusual events like the visit of a puppy or a parent, the appearance of snowfalls or thunderstorms.

I would make sure that parents are always welcome at the school. I would find out if parents are expected to stay during part of the first few days to give the child support. Can I stop in without notice? Can I occasionally share lunch with my child? If the answers to these questions are no, I'd give no more thought to this school. In order for me and my child to trust a school, I have to feel free to come and go. My child must sense that the school and I are in partnership.

I'd look closely at the space and materials. I want to find that the children can move about freely, and that there is a large play yard in use every day. I want to find materials that challenge the thinking of my child, and encourage her to create and explore. I like to see blocks, dolls, art materials, sand and water. I'm happy to find stimulating outdoor equipment like tunnels, giant boxes, steering wheels, various things to climb on and in.

If I felt comfortable with the center so far, I would then investigate the emergency procedures regarding health and fire. I'd ask about the record-keeping of children's progress, and about subsequent parent conferences. I would ask about staff turnover. I would want to know about the staff's attitudes toward families of various ethnic and racial backgrounds, and of unusual family make-up. I would be pleased to get a sense that the director is familiar with the community's resources, and that she refers families to them as necessary.

Finally, I'd trust my feelings. Is this a place where I believe my child will flourish? If I still had doubts, I would ask someone else to visit the center with me, to hear another's perspective, or I would move on to visit other centers. If I felt happy about the teachers and the general philosophy and routines, I would enroll my child with pleasure and haste. Too few caregivers have access to good preschools and daycare centers. I fervently hope that this will change. We all deserve the chance for society's children to expand and strengthen themselves joyfully.

Separation Anxiety

TEMPORARY SEPARATION

Separation is a loss, usually of a person, sometimes of an animal or object. We all experience substantial loss by the time we are three or four years old. The first, most traumatic loss is birth. We have to learn how to function without our cozy, protected environment, with its perfect, even temperature, with food coming to us without our having to communicate our need. Think for a moment of the drastic shock of that change. We start experiencing light, dark, noise; we adapt to a completely different style of satisfying our bodily needs. Our instinctive fears of loud noises and of falling come into play in those first days and weeks of this huge loss. Goodbye to the warm, quiet closeness of the womb. When we are parents, we acknowledge the trauma of our baby's birth by providing lots of our own body warmth, by speaking rhythmically and softly to our child, by providing all the nurturing we can. We are usually joyful as we bask in the newness of this little life, and so find it easy to give the new baby reassurance necessary...until we begin to tire, and our anxiety and frustration start to seep in—particularly if this is a first child.

A young child experiences other losses. She has to deal with the comings and goings of those most dear to her. For a long time she doesn't realize that those people or objects will reappear after they are gone. That is what gives the game of peek-a-boo such sharp fascination—the baby is continually surprised that the person reappears from behind the hands (peek-a-boo, incidentally, is derived from an Old English phrase meaning 'dead or alive'). Blowing out matches and candles, hiding things and finding them—all owe their charm to the lack of surety that things will come back. You have probably noticed children hiding in the same place, time after time, and loving it when you pretend you have no idea where they are hiding. These disappearances are very short losses, and help the child to experience longer and longer removals from their familiar people.

There are also losses of favorite toys and blankets, of friends as they move away, of pets, even of caterpillars and spiders a child has momentarily adopted. If her family moves, think of the losses a child sustains: room, house, neighborhood, friends, school, and all the other people and things she has come to recognize. A child must start over again, learning to know new sets of everything. Is it any wonder that children's behavior often regresses after their household moves?

Think about losses you have had in recent years. Have you given up coffee, alcohol, tea, nicotine, junk food? I have given up most of these in the past twenty years and can testify to a significant sense of loss. They were my friends.

The temporary loss of a parent is any separation for any length of time. Most caregivers need relief from parenting, and begin to think about resuming some of the parts of their lives they shelved during their child's first months and years. Once a child has come to clearly recognize and depend on her primary nurturers, she will protest their departure. Parents: remember that your own needs count, and recognize that stress on your child, in moderation and with all the love and support you can muster, is essential for growth and development. We all need repeated exposure to change, stress, tension and excitement, in varying levels of intensity. I compare the process to becoming more or less immune to colds and childhood diseases; we need to pick up enough of them inside of our bodies for us to build antibodies. Then we won't be sick all the time. We need small doses of stress to prepare us for the big ones, and we can't predict when they'll be coming our way.

I am taking aerobics, which does for my body what I am describing in children's psyches. I'm exercising with increasing intensity each day, because I want to build up my lung and heart strength. Unusual physical stress will occur to my body at some point, and I intend to be able to withstand it.

Lateesha is going to stay at a babysitter's house. The minute she and her father are in the car, Lateesha starts to scream. Her father might say, "Stop your crying. I don't know what you're crying about, you always have a good time at Carmen's. You like to play with her children." Lateesha continues to cry, and her father carries her, screaming, to Carmen's house, wondering why on earth his daughter is carrying on so.

Lateesha, who is four, is scared that her parents will not return—a common fear in young children. We need to acknowledge it. In the above scene, had the father said the words I wrote for him, her feelings would have been denied, and she would have felt even more isolated. She was worried about going to the babysitter, and her father wasn't showing sensitivity to her worries.

What did the father actually do? He wrote a note for his daughter. Lateesha can't read yet, but she was impressed by the power of the written word. Her father took out a small pad of paper and asked Lateesha what she wanted him to write. Her tears dried, and she dictated a note. It said, "I don't want you to go away. I want to stay home with you. I don't want to stay at Carmen's." Her parent took this dictation very seriously, without editorial comment. He wrote exactly what Lateesha said, read it back to her, and then gave it to her for safekeeping.

At Charlie Mills Preschool, we have found that children respond enthusiastically to the use of notes for all sorts of situations, usually those involving sadness and fear about separation. After a parent has left—if it is particularly difficult for the child to let the parent go—we may say, "Would you like me to write you a note?" The child almost always wants to dictate a note. Perhaps she'll say, "I want my mommy. I want my daddy. I want my doggy." We read it back, sign the child's name, and give it to her, and she folds it up and puts it into her pocket. The child feels that we have given proper attention to her feelings; we have dignified them by putting them on paper. In a sense, we have put her feelings to rest, and she can go about her business, feeling secure that we know how she feels.

Feelings lie dormant. Often a child has successfully managed the period of separation from a parent, with or without a note. Then comes a time, later in the day, when those feelings surge through her. It may happen because the child is less involved with activities for the moment, and therefore has a chance to think about her worries, or because the child has a difficult encounter with another child and longs for her strongest defender, her parent. You might need a second note, containing the same general message without comment by the teacher, except to read it aloud as written. The temptation might arise to point out how much fun she's having here, and to say, "You don't need your mommy." This would bring on a flood of tears, because the child would feel tricked. She would feel that you started to acknowledge her feelings, but then denied them.

The power of the written word is strong for most of us. Don't we have a certain sense that a thing is serious, and probably true, if we see it in print? Young children have already picked up that tendency, even before they can themselves write or read. When something they have said appears on paper, it is like a magic potion.

One three-year-old at school managed on most days to hold back missing his parents until lunch time; then he would collapse in tears. We arranged for him to carry a note in his pocket, sometimes from the teacher and sometimes from his mom, saying that she loved him. When tears would start to stream down his face, we would say, "You can take your note from your pocket and read it to yourself." He would do just that. He would hold the well-worn note in front of his eyes, and soon the tears would slow, and stop. He would carefully refold the note and put it back in his pocket for the next time he needed it. He was able to give himself the reassurance he needed that his parents had not abandoned him.

Children have so many fears. The more children can free themselves from dependence on adults to give them sustenance, the stronger and more independent they grow.

THE FIRST DAY OF PRESCHOOL

Every child needs the close attention of at least one person, and builds strong bonds with that person. It may not be easy for the child and parent to separate from each other when it's time to start going to a preschool or day-care center. Either or both of them may have difficulty. If they go to a school with sensitive staff, they will get some help. The adult and the child both will probably stay the first day, for a shortened period, and the duo themselves will decide how many days this will go on. In some instances, one or the other may need many days to make the break with reasonable comfort; for others, a few days is all that's necessary. The parent may need to talk about his or her unexpected feelings of fear ("no one can take care of this child like me," her father, for example, may say), and may recognize the common need to feel needed. These are normal feelings, and if the staff is supportive, the parent will be more able to trust them to care for the child.

Children need the same respect and consideration. They need to gradually learn to trust these new adults, and know it's acceptable to cry when the parent leaves. A child needs to be able to trust that her parent won't sneak away, and may stay glued to her parent if she suspects that this will happen.

The child will eventually move away and try out a few materials. Don't take that as a sign to leave. If you leave then, your child will say to herself, "If I act as though I like it here, my dad will leave. I better stick close." In fact, the staying of the parent greatly benefits both of you. You've probably not had the opportunity to observe your child from a little distance and new insights will be born as you watch the way your child deals with this new place.

When both teacher and parent feel that the child can tolerate a brief time without the parent, the parent tells the child he will be leaving for a short time, and will come back soon. Some parents have trouble saying this with confidence, and might tack on the words "all right?". Children sense any sign of uncertainty on the parent's part. Asking the child if it's all right for him to leave is giving the decision right back to the child; if you do leave at that point, the child understandably feels that you aren't listening. I often role-play a difficult leaving scenario with parents, demonstrating a short, clear, reassuring, positive, non-ambivalent message, and then leaving.

When the parent has left, I often put a comforting arm around the child, ready to accept whatever she says or does. If she cries, I let her know I understand that she misses her parent already. "I know you miss your father. You'd like him to be here right now." And then I stop talking. I only want to reflect this child's feelings back to her.

The child might say, "I hate my father!" and a teacher can respond, "You are really angry at him for leaving you here." When the sobbing subsides, the teacher may lead the child into an activity, staying close. Many people think children can be distracted from their feelings, but I disagree. Tears are the discharge of feelings, and having cried them, the child can get on with life.

This father should not stay away very long. Maybe he's in another part of the building, where the staff can phone him and report how things are going. Even if the child is actively involved in something, it's important that the separation not be too long. Each child and each parent is different, so there are no ready rules for orchestrating the delicate maneuverings that gradually lead children into their independence.

I remember a woman who seemed to have more trouble than her son with their parting. The boy, of course, sensed her reluctance, and grabbed on to it. She stayed most of each day for over a month, first playing with her child, later reading a book, but always available to him. She needed lots of support from the teachers, and she felt funny being the only parent still there. Finally, her son told her she no longer needed to stay. At our suggestion, she returned early and ate lunch with us.

Much later the woman talked with us about how hard that period had been for her, and about her doubts about the process being worth it. She was very glad that she had worked through the situation, and she told us that when her son went on to kindergarten the following year, his separation was smooth and easy. She appreciated the investment we all had made in the feelings she and her son carried.

Many children need a little help with separation every day. Some easily let their parents go with a simple, cheery goodbye, and others need a few minutes of their parents' undivided attention in the classroom. When parents and teacher can acknowledge the need, whatever it may be, the child has a much easier time.

I remember a woman who was exemplary in her sensitivity to her child. She dressed and fed her two children at home, and then brought her older daughter Tanya to school. She acted as though her morning had been a breeze, and as though she had no place to go from here. She played with Tanya every morning for about ten minutes; her daughter then let her mother go with a wave and a smile. We have a waving window where children, often with a teacher, wave goodbye to their adults if they want to, and watch them walk down the long hall to the front door. If Tanya's mother didn't stay the usual amount of time, she protested vigorously. Her mom would say, "I'm sorry; you're right, it's not time for me to go," and lovingly give her daughter a few more minutes of her time. It was then easy to leave. If she had instead said grudgingly, "Oh, all right, if you really think I need to stay," Tanya would not have felt so loved, and consequently had such as easy time giving her up.

I always phone a parent if I've noticed a stormy separation. I estimate how long it will take them to get to work or home, and call to tell them how the child is doing. I know how heartbreaking it can be to leave while your child is screaming for you. The child usually quiets down as soon as the parent is out of sight. The child's message is, "How can you possibly leave me here without you? I need you!" When the parent isn't there to hear, the child recognizes that it is pointless to continue. She may cry for a few more minutes to discharge her pain at the separation, and then pull herself together to join the group. The parents are reassured to know that the child has recovered from her pain.

REUNION PROTEST

When parents come to pick up their child at the end of the day, they're often surprised to be met with something called "reunion protest." The child says, "I'm not ready to leave." The parent may think, "Isn't this lovely. My child is so well adjusted to school, she doesn't want to leave." We interpret it differently. We think that sometimes the child is angry at being left, and punishes her parent by acting as though she is not interested in the arrival of the parent. We encourage the parent to let the child know how happy he or she is to see her, even though the end of the day is hard for tired parents and tired children. We might suggest the parent try to stay a little longer in the morning in order to remove the need for the protest.

I left my own young children with my mother for a weekend. I felt comfortable because they were with her, my own competent, loving parent. At the end of the trip I yearned for the sight and touch of my children, and, as we approached the front door, I could hear all three of them playing and laughing in the living room. I threw open the door and called out, expecting them to leap into my arms. They turned around, took one look at me, and resumed their game. I was crushed. Didn't they love me? Was I a terrible mother? They gradually warmed up to me, and I began to put it together. They hadn't liked my leaving them, even though they had had a spectacular time with their grandmother. To express their anger, they used what was available to them; the weapon of indifference.

Understanding what is going on in our children's minds at the time of reunion helps us accept their feelings. We don't need to meet their anger or indifference with anger or indifference; we can accept it and understand it. I could have said to my children, "I'm sure glad to be home with you. I missed you. I'll bet you are mad that we didn't take you with us." I could have given them each a hug, and then waited until they felt like approaching me.

Parents' most demanding job is figuring out what their children are thinking and feeling, and reacting to the actions these thoughts and feelings cause. Such maturity on our parts is rarely easy. Being an effective and loving parent involves striving for that maturity.

On the trip home from school, parents are eager to hear about their children's day. Children often react poorly to questioning, and respond reluctantly. "What did you do in school today?" "Just played." "Nothing;" "We read some books." It's difficult for children, who are creatures of the moment, to remember much of what they did. More importantly, though, most children treasure having a place of their own that they feel they don't have to share with their families, and regard much questioning as prying into this private place. Information will sift out if we are patient. Some parents very carefully ask one specific question. "What did you have for snack today?" or "Do you remember what story you heard today?" This focuses the child's attention on a particular part of the day, and she may be happy to tell about it. At times, children feel important sharing information about their day. The parent might tell the child a little bit about the parent's day; the child will feel included, and glad that her parent wants to share with her.

We keep communication open with the parents of the children at our center. We have slots for notes to parents; we might write "Please be sure to ask me about the fall Rico had on the playground today," or "I need to tell you about Joyce's continuous crying today."

Years ago I heard a talk by Prof. James Hymes about home/school relations. He said that he thought all parents brought some fear of teachers to their child's classroom, and suggested that all of us were somewhat afraid of teachers when we were small. They were big, powerful people who judged us, determined our promotions, and ran our lives for years. Hymes thinks that we retain that feeling about teachers, and that this gets in the way of our relating as well as we could to our children's teachers. I'm inclined to agree with him. When teachers acknowledge that parents are doing the very best they can for their children, parents will be more able to trust them. When parents work to understand the stresses of teachers, they are more ready to give that trust. Both must work hard. Our children's lives depend on us.

Privacy and Autonomy

Young children live in a world of giants. The furnishings of the giants' houses are built for people twice the children's height. Small people have to climb to get onto a couch, let their feet dangle from chairs, and need stools to reach the toilet. They have to climb on a chair to get to kitchen cabinets. Only their cribs and high chairs are built with their size in mind. In the world of giants, young children stand in the position of supplicants, needing help to exist, and gazing up at the chins of adults. Children recognize the undersides of tables more than they do the surfaces that hold the world's things.

In places built for young children, furniture is geared to their size. The pace is built on their rhythms. Adults stoop to be at the level of children, and materials are chosen to fit the abilities of the inhabitants. These particular grown-ups, cognizant of the leaps and pitfalls of early childhood, expect things appropriate to the children. Places built with these occupants in mind are called preschools.

There are countless reasons for preschools, all the reasons springing from real situations at home. There is no one there to care for the child. There are few other children in the neighborhood to play with the child. The caregiver at home needs time for him or herself. The child is so difficult that grown-ups hope that a preschool will straighten her out. The private school the parents hope to enroll their child in later demands a particular preschool as a qualification for enrollment. The child needs an atmosphere of enrichment.

Preschool can be a child's first real private life. At preschool she has friends and experiences unknown to her parent. At pick-up time, her adult may question her. Maybe the child really did nothing, or maybe she's withholding something important from her caregiver. Parents may tend to push harder then, asking more questions, and may come up against a privacy-protecting obstinacy that surprises them.

Adults can learn to respect the privacy of their children. A child feels important having a world of her own. If not quizzed, she will offer tidbits of information from time to time. If she can tell of school when she wants to and where she wants to, she's likely to give more details. When we don't know what to say to a child, we often ask questions: "What is your name? How old are you? Where do you go to school?" We are uncomfortable trying to get into a child's world, so we put them on the spot. We direct the conversation; often it's an interrogation.

Parents can greet their children with statements. "I'm glad to see you;" "I've missed you;" "I painted the bureau while you were at school, and I'm eager for you to see it." The child feels free to respond to her parent's warmth, and to offer, if she wants, information about her day. Such a greeting respects privacy, and having a private place gives a child a chance to grow in ways of her own. Her teachers and classmates have no preconceived ideas of who she is, and have no history with her. She is treated differently than she is at home. At school there are no siblings to demand attention. The demands of other children at school don't sound so strident in the ears of the child as do the cries of her brother and sister. Here she can be her own person, and try out new behavior. When her parents visit the school, or stop by to eat lunch with her, they can demonstrate their respect for her environment by asking her about the rules, and by following her lead. Their child has the advantage of being with adults who are not her parents, and who know what is appropriate for her age. She may be allowed to do things she may not do at home, or she may be prevented from doing things allowed her at home. Preschool challenges the child. She learns what is acceptable there.

A child should gradually feel safe at preschool. In the nurturing environment of a good center, she can grow in whatever ways she needs. Some children need to learn to be more assertive, and some less so. Some need to feel comfortable expressing their thoughts, and others to listen and stand back more. Some need to gain the confidence to take risks, and others to develop appropriate caution. Each can grow into her own private world, separate in key ways from the identity her parents have given her, and able to build on the support of her family. It's a special place.

Parents often find it difficult to give children independence and at the same time give them the security of knowing that parents are in charge. It's an extremely delicate balance, and most of us worked long and hard to establish it. Balance is vital. When children resist the imposition of limits, parents may worry, questioning their own reasoning and methods. All children need clear limits. They test them to find out how firm they are, where they stop, when they apply. Young people need to know that stronger, wiser people are responsible for their well-being. If children think they themselves are running the show, they get anxious, and look at every turn for sensible limits.

Eating is a stellar example of conflict in families, and can be an example of clarity in limits. Parents think they should dictate eating habits, and children often think they should decide. Childhood conflict over meals can grow into eating disorders later in their lives (adults spend millions on diet books and diet pills). Let's look at the opportunity mealtimes give us to practice clarity.

Parents may overestimate a child's appetite, putting more on her plate than she can eat. As an adult I've occasionally been served a huge plate of spaghetti and subsequently lost my appetite. The portion was so big that I was overwhelmed, and didn't even want to begin it. Small servings are appropriate for small people.

Locked in eating conflicts with my second child, I came upon a paragraph in a book suggesting that I measure the food I put on his plate. I was shocked at the amounts I had been dishing out. For some weeks I gave him only a tablespoon of each food. Before long, instead of resisting the serving, he was asking for seconds. I'd been worried that he was not eating enough (and that I was therefore not a good parent). The two of us had become caught in a painful, daily struggle. He could easily win, simply by not eating as much as I thought he ought to. Once I left him the choice, starting the meal with tiny servings, he ate more. He took charge, and could ask for more if he wanted it. This was an eye-opener for me, and I realized that there are times when my child could easily be the leader.

We can encourage autonomy in many other areas, looking carefully at who sets the limits, and who needs them, our children or us. We can resist the urge to do everything for our children, and we can help them when they truly need it. We have to be willing to watch a child struggle and fumble. We need, as always, to take the long view, and admire the process rather than the result. If Mary puts on her shirt by herself, whether or not it is backward, she has taken a step in dressing herself. We overlook its backwardness. "You struggled and you did it!" If we're pushed by time and by circumstances, we may take over for the child. If we do, we can be conscious of our reasons, and honest about them.

"Since we need to leave for daycare in five minutes, I'm going to put your shirt on for you today. In the car, you can put on your boots by yourself, and tell me what kind of shirts you like the most." When we can, we may start her dressing time a few minutes earlier, so that she can develop the ability to dress herself.

Whose power is important in a case like this? The reality is that a parent often decides what will happen, and often this is highly appropriate. When we can keep our hands off while our child struggles, her feeling of triumph when she masters the task can reward us. We see her pleasure, and we can look forward to more and more of our own freedom as she learns to take care of herself. We can be successful teachers and confident parents.

Part Two

Behavior

CAUSES OF BEHAVIOR

"Rolf is driving me crazy. He hits his sister, he has tantrums, he won't eat at mealtimes. I can't stand him!" When a child misbehaves, it's useful to figure out the cause. (There is always a cause.) When we find it, we have a chance to change the child's behavior.

Brainstorming is one way to do the detective work necessary. Each parent or teacher speaks whatever comes to mind, not censoring ideas, not commenting on others' ideas. When all the possibilities have been jotted down, look at them thoughtfully. You'll discard most, but one or two may hit a nerve. You may suddenly realize that you can probably pinpoint what is bothering her, and yet you never thought of it before. Brainstorming loosens one's mind, and helps us express ideas that more thoughtful discussion might inhibit.

Keeping a diary is another method of searching for the cause of behavior. We write down what and when the child eats, when she sleeps, her activities and playmates and whatever else seems pertinent. We mention the times when the objectionable behavior occurs. After a few days, we look at the written record of the child's recent life. Sometimes a causal connection quickly emerges. Maybe each meal containing eggs brings on a tantrum. The parent eliminates eggs from the child's diet, and the tantrums stop. Parents often find it difficult to believe that food allergies can cause dramatic behavior changes. Allergists have demonstrated the connection to my satisfaction. If food doesn't appear to be the problem, note whether tantrums follow late bedtimes or contact with a particular playmate or adult. Careful analysis may give you a clue.

Parents may feel they don't have time to keep a diary; they have all they can do to keep up with the daily chores and heartaches of parenting. But dealing with objectionable behavior also takes a lot of time and energy. In the long run, you'll feel more relaxed if you can help your child modify her behavior. I compare the process of keeping a diary to putting money in the bank: hard to save at the time, delightful later when you get the interest. A parent receives, as interest, more pleasurable time with the child, and spends less time and energy attempting to correct undesirable behavior.

Last year three-year-old Danny came to our school. Danny's father had been away from home for almost a year. One day Danny's mother told us that her husband would be returning home in a few weeks. Immediately we began to see changes in Danny's behavior; he no longer focused easily on activities; he couldn't play comfortably with other children; he often threw himself on the floor, his laugh bordering on hysteria. Formerly an easygoing, adaptable child, Danny had become one of the most difficult to handle. What was going on in his mind?

Danny knew that his father would be coming home soon. He was two and a half when his father left. He had only dim memories of his dad, whereas he and his mother had become a cozy twosome. Could it be that he was worried about sharing his mom with his dad? Did he worry that his father would displace him in the eyes of his mother?

If these were his worries, he was probably feeling unloved and unwanted. An antidote to his feeling rejected was to receive lots of affection from his mother, relatives and teachers. We gave him extra hugs; we paid special attention to what he was doing. We often described his work to him, showing that we were aware of him and his projects and activities. It wasn't easy to be warm to him, since his actions were particularly unlovable. (I have gradually learned that the least likable child is usually the one most in need of love.) We and his mother gave each other support in continuing our love campaign. Quite quickly, Danny gave up some of his new, difficult behavior. He did not totally revert to his former delightful self, but he moderated his most bothersome behavior. Seeing the change was so gratifying that it was easier for us to continue our appreciation of him. We were getting results.

Danny's father came home. Now it was he who brought Danny to school each day. For a day or two Danny was unusually subdued. Then he became more focused, more likable, more relaxed. Soon we had the old lovable Danny back. Even if our analysis hadn't been particularly accurate, we acted appropriately. We tried to understand the cause of his behavior change and then acted on our analysis. What we chose to do, give extra love and attention, would be good for him whatever the causes of his behavior.

When I'm focusing on a child's positive aspects, and when I am giving affection, I become fonder of the child. As I invested more of myself in Danny, I liked him better, and I could see more of his likable side because I was looking for it. When children misbehave, we tend to forget they have other fine qualities. Giving extra love and attention pays off. The child behaves better, the adult likes the child better, the child likes the adult better. We have made a circle of supportive behavior.

DISCIPLINE

The questions asked me most by parents concern discipline. Parents are understandably concerned with raising their children to do things properly. They want their young children to become comfortable members of their own family and of society. "Discipline" is the word most often used to describe the achievement of these goals.

There are a number of meanings of the word "discipline." One is a noun: the showing of the effects of discipline, or self-discipline. The other is a verb: to discipline one's children or dogs. Most parents and teachers believe that the noun is accomplished by practicing the verb, and that well-disciplined children are the result of discipline by the parents. I'm not sure that I fully agree with this assumption.

It's natural for parents to be concerned about the way their children behave. Their behavior affects the smoothness of the functioning of the household. It affects the way the world sees the family, and the future competence and happiness of children is closely related to their behavior. I agree that it is very important to find ways to affect the behavior of children. It's the method of influencing them that I question.

Discipline is usually broken into two parts: punishment and reward. A multitude of books on this subject describes different ways of administering these two. Punishment is discussed using words like natural consequences, logical consequences, firmness, occurring immediately after bad behavior, consistent, done not in anger but with love. It is said that children need (and, deep down, really want) punishment to keep them in line. However, research that impresses me shows that punishment does little to permanently affect behavior, except to make children defiant and resentful of the power exerted by their parents. Punishment is a humiliating use of power.

Rewards are the flip side of punishment. Rewards are gifts given by the parent in an effort to enhance what they consider positive behavior. A grown-up with power tells the child she may have a longer recess for being quiet in school, or may stay up later as a reward for being so good to her little sister. Rewards and punishment have a temporary effect. They don't permanently change a young child's behavior in the ways the controller hopes.

Aren't we seeking, in fact, *self*-discipline? What we really want is intrinsic control, not imposed control. We want children to behave in appropriate ways because it makes sense to them, not because of what someone else says. The student who studies because she is excited and interested learns more than the one who studies for a grade. The child who gets along well with her little sister because it is more pleasant for her will develop into a grown person who knows how to relate comfortably and with satisfaction, and who knows how to survive the give and take of relationships. She'll be more socially adapted than a child who doesn't hit her little sister because she fears punishment.

When a controlling parent isn't around, a child has less motivation for proper behavior. When a strict teacher leaves the classroom momentarily, the class may explode. When a teacher who has helped the class find joy in concentrated work steps out for a moment, there is less difference in the atmosphere. The young people are not being quiet from fear of their teacher but because they are engrossed in their work.

Let's imagine a family meeting where chores are being discussed. One of the parents starts listing jobs that seem essential: cooking, setting the table, cleaning, dishwashing, laundry, trash, shopping. A child adds, "feeding the dog." A discussion ensues; how should the jobs be allocated? Should they be rotated? The group eventually decides that each person will choose a job until all are taken. In some cases, two work together on one job. During the meeting, the adults work hard at not dominating, because it's important for the children to be equally involved in this process. If you've chosen to do a particular job, they believe, you are more likely to follow through than if it were imposed on you.

How does the first week unfold under this new democratic system? On the second day, the parents become aware that Mary has not fed the dog at the usual time. They decide to let the dog remind her, instead of doing it themselves. Much later, Mary is about to go to bed when she sees Spot carrying his feeding dish all around the apartment. She says, "Oh, Spotty, I bet you're hungry. I nearly forgot to feed you." She happily puts food in his dish, ruffles his fur, and goes to bed. You can imagine the scene avoided by the parents' restraint; nagging, resisting, procrastination, more nagging and recriminations.

How often we take responsibility away from our children when we really want them to accept it. Suppose the trash is piling up in the kitchen. Trash is Benny's job. His father might say, "I find it hard to work in the kitchen when the trash is spilling out onto the floor." This is a statement of how the father feels, not a direct request to Benny. Since he hasn't been nagged, but has heard the inconvenience his dad is feeling, Benny is more likely to say, "Gee, Dad. I'm sorry. I got so busy I forgot to take it out. I'll do it right now."

Statements with a prominent "you" in them usually charge another person with something: "You never remember to take out the trash;" "Are you lazy? You never help around the house." Sentences with "I" don't usually charge another, but state how the behavior affects *us*. We don't have to feel attacked. We can react voluntarily, and feel less pressure. Anger and resentment are not necessarily stirred.

LIMITS AND ALTERNATIVES

All of us need to know at least our rough limits; we're generally uncomfortable if we don't. Children are the same. They need to know that someone older and wiser is in charge. They are anxious if they don't see this happening. They have periods when they constantly test those limits. Don't be fooled by them. They may appear to be rejecting limits; what they're actually doing is making sure that the limits are there. They are making sure that you are in charge. Then they can relax and use their energy for other vital parts of their primary task: growing up.

How can we set reasonable limits? First, decide whether or not our expectations of children are realistic; are we expecting behavior that is too adult? Have we learned what is appropriate behavior for children of various ages? If you are experiencing a period of lots of conflict with your child, can you separate what are the most important areas to work on? None of us functions at our best if someone is constantly nagging us. We can deal with one or two issues at a time, not more.

If you've isolated the things that distress you most, you're ready to proceed. It's important to be sure that you're giving your child enough positive reactions to the things that *are* going well. That will help her feel good about herself. The most important single principle is that any consequence must logically follow the child's action. Children who write on the walls, for instance, can expect to have to clean them.

Whenever possible, children should be encouraged to think of alternate solutions, and to consider what the outcome might be. A child wants a book another has, and knocks down the child to get it. "I can tell you really wanted that book. What are some other ways you could have used to get it, so that Peter didn't end up so mad at you?" When children offer possibilities, it's important to accept all of their ideas, and not to judge them. We're trying to encourage creative problem-solving, and even ideas that seem extremely unusual just might work. We aren't focusing only on the present problem, but also on young people's growing skill at solving problems, so they can take over more and more of the responsibility for their actions.

Time-outs are popular with some parents. They shouldn't be used as punishment, however, since it isn't teaching them anything. (They pay their fine, and resume as before.) They are useful, though, when a child has lost control, and cannot deal with reason at that moment, or when two children need to be separated. Time-outs can give a child the chance to calm down before talking with the parent. We often make the mistake of trying to reason with a child who is in the grip of strong emotion. We know, from our own experience, that when our feelings are powerful we may not think well. We all need time to calm down, and time-outs can help. Some behavior is best treated by ignoring it. Sometimes children are trying to get our attention by doing something they know we disapprove of. If we reprimand them, they have succeeded in getting our attention. Some behavior eliminates itself if we pay no attention to it. You'll see for yourself which things respond to such treatment, and which you are comfortably able to ignore.

In disciplining children, remember that our goal is to teach. If we try something over and over again, and no change is forthcoming in our child's behavior, we try something else. We aren't asking children to pay for their misdeeds, but to learn more effective ways of handling themselves, and to become more comfortable with self-discipline.

Power

THIN AS A MARBLE

From *Love Against Hate*, by Karl Meninger:

"How the child feels about even the most reasonable requirements of civilization could be attested by child psychiatrists and child psychologists in thousands of instances; but in all the clinical literature I know of nothing so eloquent as the story brought to national attention a few years ago in the most unexpected place, the columns of *The New Yorker* (July 1, 1939). I quote it without change and without comment:

"A young mother we know has sent us a song, or a chant, or poem, or something that her four-year-old son made up and sings every evening in his bathtub. It goes on practically forever, like the Old Testament, and she was able to copy down only part of it, but even this fragment seems to us one of the handsomest literary efforts of the year, as well as another proof that children are the really pure artists, with complete access to their thoughts and no foolish reticence. It is sung, she says, entirely on one note except that the voice drops on the last word in every line. We reprint it here because seldom, we think, has the vision of any heart's desire been put down so explicitly:

"He will just do nothing at all.

He will just sit there in the noonday sun.

And when they speak to him, he will not answer them,

because he does not care to.

He will stick them with spears and put them in the garbage.
When they tell him to eat his dinner, he will just laugh at them.
And he will not take his nap, because he does not care to.
He will not talk to them, he will not say nothing.
He will just sit there in the noonday sun.
He will go away and play with the Panda.
He will not speak to nobody because he doesn't have to.
And when they come to look for him they will not find him.
Because he will not be there.
He will put spikes in their eyes and put them in the garbage.
And put the cover on.
He will not go out in the fresh air or eat his vegetables.
Or make wee-wee for them, and he will get thin as a marble.
He will do nothing at all.
He will just sit there in the noonday sun."

"Most people do not remember having had such feelings in child-hood, or remember them only dimly."

"For when emotions are stimulated which it is dangerous to express outwardly, their suppression is gradually replaced by repression, that is, by denying the experience and then excluding it from consciousness and from conscious memory."

[Author's note: Pete Seeger made a song of this work and sings it on one of his records.]

Young children, in general, feel powerless. Sometimes we, as adults, also feel that we have little power, but children are always a rung lower than we are. They are small in size, living in a world that was made for adults, and they have very little say in how their lives are carried out. They are often ridiculed; people tell them what they've done wrong and not what they've done right; they are accorded little dignity; others invent the routines they must follow. They're told when to get up, when to go to bed, what to eat and how to eat it, when to use the toilet, how to speak and to whom. They are taken to lessons or programs or camps or clubs whether or not they enjoy them.

Most grown-ups would be surprised if they were to learn that young children often want their parents to be flung into the garbage can and the cover put on. Parents often say, 'You don't mean that." The child knows she means it at that moment, and might then feel invalidated on top of everything else.

How can parents guide and instruct their children and still not make them subjects? Allow them their feelings. It's all right to be angry or sad or resentful, sometimes to hate your parents or your brothers or your teacher. Feelings are important. "I know that you're mad at me because I won't let you watch that television show. It is all right to be angry at me, although I won't let you hit me. You can tell me how you feel." Imagine the relief a child feels when she is understood.

In our great wisdom we want to save children from their mistakes, even though mistakes are probably the first great teacher. We had an opportunity to try something, and it didn't work. We look around for other solutions; we push our creativity. Does it really matter if your child wears mismatched socks? Maybe nobody will notice. Maybe everybody will notice, and she'll remember that she didn't like their response. Maybe she'll start a fad. If children are given freedom to make small mistakes, they are less likely, later, to make disastrous ones.

I try to allow young children the freedom to call on any and all of their own resources whenever I possibly can. I also try to use my power as an older, bigger person and a person with explicit authority over them only when necessary and only to the degree that is necessary. If children constantly take orders from us, they have no practice in making decisions. I let them know that I appreciate and respect their efforts, and that I'll comply as often as possible with the decisions they make.

PLAYING

When adults and young people play together, adults usually lead the play. They are in charge. They have the ideas; they have the power. They plan the time; they say when the time is over. Even when a child chooses the activity, the parent generally takes a lead role. I have occasionally seen parents take the back seat in play, and noticed the resulting growth in the child's self-esteem.

A man and a girl climb into a sandbox. The parent does not start talking; he watches the actions of his child, and then copies them. Anita starts to dig a big hole. Her father starts to dig a big hole. Anita says, "I'm making this really deep." Her father says appreciatively, "I see you are!" and continues digging. Anita puts a stone in the hole and buries it. He copies. Anita is absorbed in the work, occasionally glancing to see what her father is doing. They feel companionable, and are each working. More objects are buried, dug up, reburied. Her father always stays a little behind, not contributing ideas and not taking over. Anita says, "Let's make a flag." He says, "How do you think we can do that?" She finds a stick and a leaf and makes a flag. He says, "You figured out how to make a flag." He doesn't praise the product, as in "What a wonderful flag." He describes what happened. Anita found a solution. She can give her own messages to herself, or to him: "I know how to do things." Self-messages are more meaningful and more lasting than lavish praise strewn by an adult. The building and digging continue, Anita having the ideas and her father following. If they hear a call to supper, the two builders might walk hand in hand, and Anita might say, "We had fun, Daddy. Can we do that again?"

What a delightful feeling for a child. She is in charge! She has a chance to experiment without judgment. The life of this child and parent can proceed without the power struggles that dominate so much of family life. What an easy thing for a grown-up to do, and how hard it is for so many of us.

Young children don't have many opportunities to make important decisions, so they wrest power from adults in manipulative ways. They may whine and whine until an exhausted parent gives in. They pretend not to hear refusals after a clear request or warning to stop. They act as though they're helpless so that they can enslave their parents, who then end up doing everything for them. Or they behave so obnoxiously that the adult gives up and lets them have their way.

Most often, a child cares more about gaining power than about winning the particular point. We need to help them find ways of feeling legitimately powerful.

Mammoth power struggles involve dressing, eating and bathing. I find it helpful to offer two choices whenever I can. "Are you going to wear your blue shorts or your green shorts today?" "Would you like potatoes or rice for supper?" "It's almost time for a bath. Do you want your animals or your boats in the tub? And do you want a ten-minute bath or a twenty-minute bath?" (I suggest a timer for ending all sorts of activities; you can't argue with a timer.)

Without parameters, choices are too difficult for young children, and you may get answers you can't live with. When I offer choices, I take the deal seriously, and go along with the choice. If you say "Do you want to eat your supper or don't you!" be prepared for the latter. In the grocery store, a question like "Do you want to behave, or go home?" may well elicit "Go home." If that isn't your intent, and you hoped to scare your child into submission, you're in an awkward place. Children learn quickly when parents don't say what they mean. The conclusion they draw is to do whatever they want to do and ignore their ineffective parent.

The mother of three-year-old Renaldo, an effective parent, told me this story. She had been talking to him about being nice. She had told him that it hurt her when he was nasty to her, and it hurt her when she was nasty to him. She proposed that they both become nicer to each other. Later that day they were out with friends and Renaldo was showing off his vocabulary of curses. On the way home, she said to him, "It is not all right for you to use those words. I won't tolerate it. If you use them again I won't take you to visit my friends." Renaldo smiled up at his mother and said, "Now you're being a nice mother." She was startled, and had to think for a minute until she realized what he meant. He recognized that his mother was taking the reins, and was not going to let him get away with inappropriate behavior so he called her "a nice mother!" I've rarely heard a clearer image of a child asking for limits, even when superficially he seems to be trying to avoid them.

A parent knows better than a child the consequences of most actions, and has the responsibility to use this knowledge to protect the child. Daddy knows that Ann will be tired and cranky if she doesn't get enough sleep. She doesn't know this. Therefore it's the father's responsibility to see that she goes to bed early enough to ensure a good night's sleep.

Tom is unlikely to know that he will need a jacket at his day-care center. Young children are creatures of the moment. They can't predict how they will feel at another time or in different circumstances. It's warm now. He doesn't realize that it will probably be colder later, when he's outside.

It isn't fair to give choices when an answer is not in the best interests of the child. I don't ask if he wants to wear a jacket, or when she wants to go to bed. Children, living as they do in the present, will choose immediate gratification.

When parents pick up children at our center, I occasionally hear "It's time to go now, all right?" They don't mean to be offering a choice; they mean to soften the blow. The response is usually "I just want to do one more thing." Some parents have figured out how to avoid this. "My, I'm glad to see you. Today we have time to stay five more minutes if you want to." Or "I've missed you a lot. I'm glad to see you. Today we have to leave right away to go to the grocery store." The parent can hug the child, call goodbye to the teacher, and take the child's hand, using bodily movements to reinforce the message.

Young children know whether parents mean what they say. They struggle when they sense indecision on the part of the parent. Parents need to be ready to reinforce their statements, without being defensive. The child says, "My gosh. Yesterday we stayed a lot longer." "That's right, we did stay longer. Today, we can't." If the parent starts offering reasons in defense, a child knows the parent is not on solid ground, and will start the attack. Such contests don't end well for either participant. The parent has lost because the discussion has escalated to a struggle.

Parents often use too many words when they anticipate a struggle. Children need their parents to be clear, honest and simple in their statements. There certainly are times when long, thoughtful explanations are in order. It's not when parent and child are engaged in the routines of their daily lives. At such times, explanations aren't listened to. My motto is, if in doubt, use fewer words.

PARENTS IN CHARGE

Three-year-old Jonathan and his mother are shopping at the grocery store. Jonathan howls and jumps up and down, screaming for a candy bar. She doesn't believe in giving candy to children, nor does she believe in giving in to children having tantrums. Nevertheless, she's embarrassed by his noise and too tired to think about how to stop it. She gives him a candy bar.

What's happening here? Jonathan has learned how to spot his mother's vulnerable moments, and can usually bend her to his will. He has tried, to no avail, to use the same tactics with his grandmother. She, however, is able to hold out, so Jonathan doesn't try it anymore when he's with her.

It's very difficult to take the long view when your every waking moment appears to be devoted to your children. Jonathan's mother realized that she simply could not allow his manipulation any longer. The next time, she said to him, "You know that I don't give you candy because it is not good for you. I will give you an apple when we get home, or a banana in the car when we leave here. Which would you like?" She has made it very clear. Jonathan is not going to get candy. He was given a choice, a chance to have some legitimate power. He had to stop to think about this, to decide how he was going to exercise that power.

Young children need to have opportunities for honest power, when they can clearly be in charge. A parent leaving a child with a baby-sitter says, "I'm leaving now, and you can tell the baby-sitter when you want to have your bath, as long as you're in bed by eight o' clock."

Telling Children the Truth

TRUST CHILDREN, AND THEY WILL TRUST YOU

I spoke the other day with my friend Hal, who was extremely upset. His brother-in-law had been diagnosed with cancer, and he didn't know what to say to his five-year-old daughter. We discussed his possible options. We talked about the sensitivity of most children to knowing that something is going on, even if it is not spoken about. I told him that young children are so egocentric that they generally believe they are the cause of everything. Selma Frieberg speaks of this in detail in her valuable book, *The Magic Years*: If there is a divorce, they think they caused it. If someone dies, they think somehow it was their fault. If parents do not tell the child what is happening, they imagine the worst, and take full blame for it.

It's often difficult for parents to understand the framework in which a child is living. It's hard to believe, for instance, that a young child has little ability to understand the finality of death; it's not such a disaster to them. They don't know that the person won't return, and are not necessarily traumatized. It is always hard for us to put ourselves in the shoes of others; it's particularly hard to do with young children, because they see things so differently than we do. We tend to become confused, because they often use the same words we do, and we don't know that the words don't mean the same thing to them that they do to us.

I suggested to Hal that he simply tell his daughter that her uncle was very sick, and that the family was worried about him. He was still not satisfied with this answer. His discomfort was so great that he could not imagine such a simple solution. He was concerned about worrying her. He wanted to spare her from grief.

43

Hal called again the next day. It had been decided that an operation was not feasible, and the uncle might expect to live only about six months. Now what should Hal tell his daughter? We talked about the importance of her having small doses of pain and grief, and how she had already experienced the death of a gerbil and several other animals who lived at school. This had been a form of inoculation. Now she was going to get a stronger dose: a human being in her extended family. All such experiences will help her when a person closer to her dies. Hal said, "But what if she sees me crying?" We talked about the fact that his daughter cries frequently, and it may bring her closer to her father to see him crying. I suggested straightforward talk to his child; he was afraid. I proposed that he try to shake off the constraints that his own life's experience had bound him in, and just talk to her from his heart, that he really knew how to do this. Although still fearful, he sighed, and said he guessed that was right. (He told me later that this experience had probably made him a fuller person.)

It amazes me to think of the numbers of situations in which we do not tell children the truth. I heard of some young children who were told that their mother had gone on a long trip, when in fact she had died. Her children sat at the window day after day, waiting for her to return from her trip. In another case, a man had died, and his widow and young son spoke hardly at all about his death. Many months later, they discovered that each had cried silently in their respective rooms at night, week after week. How sad that they could not have cried together, and shared their pain. They would probably have felt a good deal closer, and less isolated in their grief.

Some people feel that they need to be absolutely and fully truthful with their children, and tell them, for instance, the moment they find out that they are pregnant. This kind of truthfulness seems to me unnecessary. I don't believe that you have to tell your child all you know. Parents forget what a long time nine months is. And to a young child, it is nearly endless.

When parents leave a child at school, we tell them that their parent will be back after lunch, or after the nap, or whenever they will in fact come back. We try to give them an event on which to pin the return. We talk about how much they miss their parents (and it can truly seem a great loss to a child for her parent to leave her, even for an hour or two), and how much their parents are probably missing them at this moment. We tell them only true things, though we try to measure the amount of information appropriate to give them.

Sometimes, in an effort to be truthful, people give more information than a child can absorb. This is often the case when parents talk about birth or death. They work themselves up to tell the truth, and sometimes can't stop. It is probably best to answer the questions the child asks, and little more. The same questions, or similar ones, may be asked again and again in different phases of the child's life. As a child gains more knowledge, the answers will have different meanings to her, and the parent will usually explain somewhat differently. There is the story of the child who came in to his mother's bridge group and asked where he came from. She, feeling that it is always important to tell the truth, stopped the bridge game and gave a long explanation of the birth process. When she was finally through, he shrugged and said, "Shucks, I thought I came from Boston."

There are many less dramatic times when it is important to tell the simple truth. When a baby-sitter is expected, the child should know this, even though she may be asleep before the parents leave. She might wake up and feel betrayed if she hadn't known her parents would be gone.

What do you do if you are leaving the child with a sitter, and the child is screaming? You don't let yourself be manipulated by the screaming. You calmly tell your child goodbye, hug her, and reiterate that Margaret will be staying with her until you return. You can be comforted by the knowledge that her tears will almost certainly subside the moment you have left the house.

Parents need to examine their behavior periodically to see what they are demonstrating for their children to practice. Often a parent may find that she or he is actually lying to the child. Yet what an uproar this adult will make if it is discovered that the child is lying.

What you might do rather than lying is to empathize with your young child's feelings, letting her know that you understand how much she wants to do a certain thing. Let her know that her wish will be fulfilled if it is possible, but that sometimes it isn't possible. "And I know how hard it is sometimes to wait for something you want so much," you might tell her.

Most of us share a tendency to give children lots of logical reasons when the child is in the grip of strong emotions. I don't think this accomplishes what we want. We can work wonders by letting children know that we understand the depth of their feelings, and would certainly satisfy them if we could. We're on their side, not against them. Too many child/parent interactions are tugs of war, each holding firm to his or her position. If the child's wishes are appreciated and understood, and would be gratified if they could, the child can relax. "He knows how I feel. He understands me." Understanding will diffuse many struggles with your child. You will also feel good about yourself, realizing that you're a loving parent who neither manipulates nor lies.

When a child has scraped her knee, it is better to acknowledge that doctoring it will hurt, and then be over, than to say that it won't hurt. It *does* hurt. I carry on a stream of conversation all the time I am doing the thing that hurts (putting on medicine, removing a splinter). It offers both comfort and mild distraction. Then I say "Wow, I can tell that really hurt. And now it's done." "That didn't hurt, did it?" will not play well in situations when the child does indeed hurt.

When we tell the truth to our children, far fewer situations arise that cause us trouble in knowing what to say to them. When we always tell the truth, the difficulties are significantly reduced. *How* to say it might still give us pause, and knowing how much information to share may not be easy. But when we already enjoy a trusting relationship with our children, it will last, with care, for life, and we will be of great help in their growing up fully and well.

DEATH

Children can build up familiarity with death, so that when people very close to them die, they will have had some experience in this area. We can never hope to fully alleviate the pain of death, but we can hope to make it manageable, and not overwhelming.

One young child, when seeing wedding pictures of her parents, and being told that she had not yet been born, burst into tears and asked if she were dead. Another child, a wise five-year-old out to protect herself, said, "Somebody will have to bury the last person, so I'll do it." Death is not easy for children to comprehend.

Some years ago I read about a psychologist who studied a particular nursery school class in regard to the number of traumatic experiences children had during a month. He was amazed at the large number of hospitalizations, deaths of pets, divorces, family members or intimate friends moving far away, serious injuries. He began to think about inoculating children with small doses of not-too happy experiences. He encouraged the teachers to discuss these events with the children.

Just about the time I read this book, one of my school children had a series of family members die. The family came from Canada, and each death required a trip back to Quebec. After one of these trips I decided to talk with Jacques about the death. With my heart in my mouth, I said, "Gee, I'm really sorry to hear that your uncle died." Jacques, pleased that I was concerned about his family's welfare, told me many details about his uncle and about the funeral. A few weeks later a cousin died, and he again made the trip and was absent from school. On his return I told him I was sorry about the death, and he shared more information. The experience was repeated once more. I, who had rarely mentioned the word 'dead,' who had flushed dead gerbils down the toilet rather than talk with children about death, was launched on my way to talking comfortably with children about death.

Thereafter, when a school animal died, all children had the chance to look at, touch, and discuss the dead animal. Many children who had been afraid to handle the animal alive stroked the fur and touched the claws. They almost always asked who killed it. They almost always said "Let's take it to the doctor to make it well again." And they always ended up talking about a lot of other fears touched off by the talk of death.

We told parents what we were doing. Nearly all appreciated it, saying that it was a difficult subject for them to talk about with their children. A few raised questions about conflicts in religious beliefs. I told them that I had been saying, when a child introduced such issues, that people had different ideas about what happened to creatures and people who died. "Yes, some people believe such and such." One danger I considered was in the saying of such things as "God came and took him." It struck me that this was presenting a frightening aspect of whatever God different families might honor.

Since that time I have discussed death openly with hundreds of children. We have talked about the death of crickets, lizards, cats, television characters, public figures, teachers, relatives and friends. We have talked about the need to mourn. I've helped them feel that it is appropriate to be sad about the dying of a pet. I have discouraged the idea that we need to run right out and replace it. I've suggested that sometime they might get another pet, but that no living thing can be replaced.

As the director of the preschool at the Hospice, I found myself talking more about death. One year, on the first day of school, I read Margaret Weiss Brown's marvelous classic *The Dead Bird*, because a child spoke about the death of his neighbor. Before going to Hospice, I'm sure I would not have read such a book so soon, before getting to know the children better. I realize that discussion of sex is no longer taboo in our culture, but talking of death often is. I want to help children dissolve that taboo.

One of the things I have done is to let children know much more about my personal life than before. They know about my children and my parents. They personally know my husband. They know my parents are dead, but aren't able to accept the irreversibility of such a fact, and still wonder whether someday my mother might pick me up from school.

A week ago the grandmother of one of our school children died. The girl's mother was crying as she told me. I had my arm around the mother, and told her daughter, and other children, that she was crying because her mother had just died. We're often afraid of overwhelming children by sharing our grief with them, and we believe it will be too upsetting for them to see us cry. On the contrary, it is more upsetting when they know something is awry, but not what. They are likely to imagine the worst, and frequently that they are the cause of it.

All children have angry feelings about their parents at one time or another. If a parent dies, they often think they caused the death. "If I had been a better son, my mother wouldn't have died. If I'd done what she told me, she wouldn't have died." Children need to feel included in the family's mourning. If they are shut out, children are alone in struggling with their fears and terrors. How a child copes with the death of a close family member is related to the support the remaining family is able to give her, and to how much they're able to help her recognize and speak about her deepest feelings.

A father I knew was much better able to deal with the death of his wife because of his need to prepare his five-year-old son for her death from cancer. In talking about what was about to happen, and in giving the son a role in the family sorrow, the father had already begun to accept and deal with her imminent death. When the boy's mother died, several days later, the father woke the son, and they went outside to pick flowers as they had planned. They went together to the room where the woman lay, and the boy put flowers in his mother's hands. They prayed together. Not only did the father help himself, he kept the child from feeling excluded, and helped him learn that he could deal with such severe and monumental stress.

John Showalter suggests that when a parent dies the child often loses both parents: one to death and the other to mourning. Haim Ginott, in *Between Parent and Child*, says, "To adults the tragedy of death lies in its irreversibility. No one can see one's self ceasing, without a future. To children it is a mystery. Young children cannot comprehend that death is permanent. It makes the child weak and anxious, because he has believed that he can influence events by wishful thinking. In spite of tears and protests, a pet or person does not return. He feels abandoned and unloved. A parent is often asked, 'After you die will you still love me?'"

DIVORCE

Parents often believe that they should shield the child from an impending divorce. Often such a choice causes more hurt than telling, because the child makes up a scenario that fits the available, though scanty, facts. Children hear and see more than we realize. They overhear telephone conversations when they are quietly playing nearby. What they imagine is usually more frightening then the reality, and they continue to feel responsible. As with their feelings of self-blame about death, so do they worry about causing divorce or separation. "If only I had been better. If I hadn't acted so mad and stinky at Daddy, he wouldn't have left."

It helps when parents tell the child as soon as the decision is definite and absolutely clear. I remember that my father told me about an impending separation when I was six. He said that he and my mother were no longer best friends. He asked me who my best friend at camp had been that year. "Bishy," I told him. He asked me about the year before. "Stacy." He said that it was the same with him and my mother. They had changed their feelings and were not best friends any more. He explained that this meant he would be living somewhere close by. He made clear that he still loved me, and that he would see me every single weekend. I wish that he had said that it was not my fault. To this day I carry traces of the sense that I might have been able to prevent the divorce by behaving better. I know in my head that this is not true, but I feel whisperings in my heart.

Along with truth, children need consistency. The child's world is being torn apart, and she needs things to hold onto. If she is to see the absent parent on weekends, it is important that this really happen. If things do not progress as planned, the child feels responsible. When an expected visit doesn't take place, the child's feelings should be dealt with openly and honestly. One might say, "I know you are disappointed because you didn't see Mommy today. You were really looking forward to that visit, and now you are mad and sad." The child can realize that you understand her feelings and sympathize with her. Too often we are tempted to say, "Don't cry. You'll see her next week. She didn't mean to miss this visit." In saying such words, we deny the child the right to have and to express highly appropriate feelings. We're giving information instead of accepting feelings. When I'm in the grip of strong feelings, it's useful to me if someone acknowledges those feelings. I get over them sooner if I know someone else understands how I feel. Any factual information the person wants to give me can be shared later, after my feelings have been vented and acknowledged. It's a mistake to try to reason with a person who is feeling deeply. We often do that with children who are angry, but their feelings must fade before their minds can open.

Many children carry a lifelong ache about their parents' divorce. Parents needn't feel guilty about this; that's just the way it is. Most children feel a permanent loss. Knowing this should not deter parents from separating, if separating is what they need to do. Staying together for the sake of the children used to be what people thought they had to do. Too many children have grown up in severely miserable households because the parents sacrificed their own feelings in the mistaken belief that they were giving a gift to their children.

Divorce brings great stress to all involved. It's a time when everyone's feelings should be acknowledged. While it's important that children not be burdened with the intimate details of the adults' problems, they need to hear some portion of the truth, and to realize that their parents are suffering. They need to know they're not responsible for the break-up. They need clear, simple information and as much consistency as the parents can manage.

HOSPITALIZATION and
OTHER PREDICTABLE TRAUMAS

Elena, age three, is going to the hospital to have her tonsils taken out. Her parents, in the interest of sparing her anxiety, have told her nothing about it ahead of time. She is in the car, the car turns into the hospital's parking lot, and Elena's mother says, "We're going to the hospital to have your tonsils taken out."

In her short life, Elena has heard many scary things about hospitals, and remembers it vividly from when her grandpa died. She naturally starts to scream. Her mother carries her, kicking and yelling, into the hospital.

We can prevent such anguish. Let's think about how most of us react to new ideas. We often reject them, or find them frightening, either until we have time to ponder them or until we get more and better information. Children are the same. Their fantasies are usually worse than the reality. They need solid information, told with compassion and empathy, so they can deal comfortably with new, and perhaps frightening, experiences.

Let children act out upcoming traumatic situations. An adult can provide simple props to recreate a hospital scene. (A good book about hospitalizations is Sara Bonnett Stein's *The Hospital Story*). The parent can act out the fantasy operation with the child, correcting some of the mistaken ideas which the child is sure to be holding, but letting the child do as she feels like doing. The child might take each of the roles in different scenarios of the event: patient, doctor, mother, nurse. Taking on the persona of the doctor can help overcome the feelings of powerlessness that are almost always present for all of us in frightening situations. The child, in taking the dominant and active role of the doctor, will probably act in ways that are very different from a doctor's style. It's important for the parent not to criticize this, but to reflect the feelings the child is showing. "You're feeling pretty strong!" "You act like you're mad at that baby!" This is a time for the child to get straight information about what will happen, and to work out some of the inevitable fears that will come up.

The technique of playing out potentially frightening situations can be a great help in dealing with all sorts of predictable traumas: the first time a child will be left with a sitter; the first time staying overnight at another house; the first time going on a school bus; the first time going to an adult social gathering where the child will be encouraged by others to be seen and not heard. Knowing what is going to happen helps us all get used to the idea of something new.

Many hospitals give children an opportunity to visit ahead of time, and do some of the playing described above. If your hospital makes provision for this, your at-home role-playing can supplement it. Some of you may yourself believe that the less you know about something as mysterious as an operation, the better. This is not usually the case for children. We often do children an injustice by shielding them from the truth.

Self-Esteem

I met Jesse and his mother and sister in the Minneapolis airport. My plane was delayed several hours, as was his, so I had a long time to get to know him. He appeared to be about three years old. I was immediately impressed by his joyousness. He got great pleasure from everything he did. He took trash to the wastebasket, read his comic book, ate a large muffin while sitting on the floor, played with his trucks. I became aware that his mother never spoke to him in an angry voice, and never scolded him. She was always agreeable to what he was saying or asking. He wanted to walk around the airport, and she willingly joined him on the stroll. His mother walked with a crutch, so walking was not simple for her. When they returned from their inspection of the airport, they were cheerily discussing what they had seen. He and his seven-year-old sister shared a bran muffin. When he had eaten all he wanted, she suggested that he wrap the balance and take it to the trash can. He made this trip with his own leftovers, then with his sister's, and happily again with his mother's. Several times I thought to myself, "I have never seen so contented a child." He seemed to enjoy whatever he was doing. He put all of himself into each activity. He "read" a comic book for a full fifteen minutes, carefully studying each page, describing the action in detail. His ability to concentrate, his self-sufficiency and his ability to articulate all convinced me that he was three years old. Later I found out that he was a two-year-old with high self-esteem.

After an hour or so of observing him, I had an opportunity to speak with his mother. I told her how favorably impressed I was with her parenting skills; that I rarely saw a parent whose every message helped her child grow in self-esteem; that it seemed as though he and she totally enjoyed each other. To many parents, an airplane delay of three or four hours is pure torture, but to her it seemed an opportunity to share an adventure with her children. She told me that her parents had both been alcoholics, and that she felt that she had had to hold the family together. She described her childhood as one without being spoken to, only yelled at. As a young child she had determined that, if she herself had children, she would treat them very differently indeed. She succeeded. I think most people find it difficult to raise their children differently than they were themselves raised, because the primary models of parenthood are one's parents. What we know of nurturing, we learn from our own nurturing or lack of it. Abused children often abuse their children: a sad heritage. Jesse's mother had been so determined to avoid the mistakes of her own parents that she succeeded in unlearning those lessons. She invented her own ways. Her story helped me understand why she used a voice with her children that was extremely sweet, and a voice that had grated on me all the while I was basking in the relaxed and delightful environment she and her children built around me in the airport. Since she was going to talk nicely to her children, she must have told herself, then she would *really* talk nicely. I suppose her syrupy voice was the exact opposite of the screams with which she grew up. I realized, in my silent judging and appreciating of this family, that I could let go of minding her tone. She had succeeded beyond belief in what she set out to do. Her children were striking examples of children who knew they were loved, and their zest for their lives was something I rarely see. Their egos were strong; they had no reason to test for reassurance. They were comfortable in their own skins.

Later I related this story to a friend. She shared with me an experience of unusual parenting she had observed. She saw a woman shopping in the supermarket, accompanied by a young boy clinging to her cart. As my friend was leaving the store, she noticed that the boy was no longer with her, and saw his mother begin to look for him. He was discovered on the sidewalk outside the store, and his mother's relief was evident. She went outside and stooped down to talk with him, calmly explaining that it was dangerous for him to be where cars were so close and so speedy. My friend was greatly impressed with the caring way in which this woman had let her child know why his leaving her was not acceptable. She believed that he got a clear and thoughtful message, and knew that her worry, though important, did not put her love for him at risk.

I recall that one of the few times I spanked one of my children was when she had been lost. I was so full of that potent mixture of anger and relief that I spanked her hard. I don't think it helped her not get lost again. I don't think it helped our relationship, and I feel no pride in the remembering. I think, though, that it is more typical a response than the ones I cited above. I take off my hat to the mothers who act as teachers to their children, rather than as fierce disciplinarians: they make a far more useful contribution to their children's growth.

Children's Thinking

Children's minds work in different ways than do most adults. They have so much less experience in which to fit information. Therefore they take many expressions literally. Children as well as adults put current information into the framework of past experience. Our understanding is based on our lives.

The father of a four-year-old friend of mine resumed playing basketball after a lapse of some years. Several evenings a week he went off to join others for recreational basketball. His four-year-old, Spencer, kept asking, "When are we going to see Daddy on TV?" Family questioning revealed that Spencer believed his father was a professional basketball player. All Spencer knew about basketball he had learned from television. He logically assumed that his father was one of the players he would eventually see on the screen. His experience of basketball was so limited that his assumption arose from that small pile of information. When informed that his father would never be on television, Spencer was irate. He knew basketball players dribbled and shot on television and that was that! Most of us react sharply when what we believe we know is challenged. We become defensive, as Spencer did.

This fall, friends visited us for the weekend. Cold weather was forecast (the first of the season), so they packed warm clothes for the family. They drove the packed car two hundred miles and were greeted enthusiastically by us. A delightful, active weekend followed, with biking, hiking, talking and games. On Sunday afternoon when the parents began collecting their belongings, four-year-old Artie, agitated, demanded "Why are you packing the car?" His parents tried to explain to him that they soon must drive home. "But I thought we were staying all winter!" screamed Artie. After much soothing and explaining, we learned that the family's discussion of warm clothes and dressing for cold weather had caused Artie to assume they had come prepared for a long stay, probably for the winter, at least.

Young children, trying to blend new information with their scanty background, make assumptions with creativity and intelligence. In the above cases (once the misunderstanding was uncovered), the child could gradually absorb the new explanation and gain some understanding. The adults with Spencer and Artie brought patience to their talks, recognizing that the child misunderstood the situation. The parents' concern for and patience with their children's feelings and their thoughtful explanations helped reveal the situations as they really were.

Think of the number of times when such misconceptions are not uncovered! Parents and children are at odds and no one recognizes the true cause; children process information so differently than we do that we are constantly amazed. I'm often aware of how well the average six-year-old functions in the world. First grade, special school events, homework, complicated relationships and faraway trips. When I think of how little information about the world she can have absorbed in six short years, I'm surprised we don't have more misunderstandings.

It may be that many contests between adult and young child arise from assumptions based on limited knowledge. Did this child really understand what I just said? I thought I was clear, but did I really speak to her limited experience in this area? We can probably better handle such struggles if we ask the child to state her position. Once we are given some insight into her way of thinking, we can work toward clearer communication. Don't be fooled by the child's apparent ease with thought and language. Children sometimes talk as though they understand much more than they can have learned in their short stay on the planet. Sometimes our own thinking is limited more than we realize.

Sibling Rivalry

I have heard several parents of a new baby say, laughing, that they are not sure they would have had the baby if they had known what a change it would make in their household. When a couple has no children, they learn to relate to each other. They learn to respect each other's rights, and to anticipate what the other might need. Moods, idiosyncrasies, preferences, all are subjects of much discussion and controversy. Both people in the couple find ways to accommodate learning; when to give in and when to assert oneself goes on for years. No one can ever predict what changes occur in the adults' relationship when a new member is added to the family. Some say that couples never get back to their original level of intimacy until their children have grown and left home. Children take so much from the relationship because their needs are primary for such a long time. A young child has not learned to wait, so when she wants, she usually *gets*. One or the other of the parents is likely to feel slighted during the early years of rearing young children. There suddenly seems to be very little time to meet each other's needs, and the parents may feel a sense of growing apart.

Then another child comes into the family. All members reel from the shock. One might think that once a parent or set of parents has adjusted to one young person, another can be taken in stride. Not so. The family dynamics are multiplied to an incredible degree. Each parent might, for instance, without necessarily realizing it, choose a favorite. The older child has to give up the accustomed place in the sun. From being the person in the family whose needs were most readily met, this child now finds herself frequently taking a back seat.

Although the parents have assured their firstborn that they have enough love to go around, the evidence belies this. Now the parents jump when this new little being cries. Now visitors come to admire this person. Why are we surprised when the older child begins to feel neglected and rejected? The parents' interest in her seems to have shriveled. The firstborn is disturbed and confused. Attention has been equivalent to love, so she feels displaced and unloved. She does everything she can to regain the parents' attention.

It might be useful for adults to imagine this scenario: suppose your spouse comes to you and says, "You know, dear, I love you very much. You're such a delight to me. However, I'm going to bring another marriage partner into our family. You can surely understand that I have enough love to go around, and that I won't love you any less. And I am sure that you will grow to love this new member of our family. You'll have lots of company and lots of fun with this person."

Do you think that the average adult would react with pleasure and emit a glow of anticipation at the advent of this new person, gladly giving up her or his room, not to mention outgrown clothes and other possessions? Looked at in this manner, it helps us see why a young child is sometimes aggressive towards a new baby, and why a child may revert to younger behavior when a baby arrives. The child may be saying to herself, "They're paying all this attention to the baby, and the baby wets, and sucks her thumb, and drinks out of a bottle. I'll do some of these things again, and maybe they'll pay attention to me."

It is perfectly natural that a child will have ambivalent feelings towards the baby. The parents can plan to spend time alone every day with the older child. They should continue as many routines as possible that were in effect before the baby was born. They can plan special activities for the older child while the baby is nursing or sleeping. They can ask visitors to pay attention *first* to the older child. They can keep presents in reserve, and give them to her when people bring presents for the baby. They can openly discuss feelings about the interloper. They can let their older child know that, although they love the baby, they also become very irritated when it cries, or interrupts sleep. They can refrain from talking about the new baby for too long a time before it is born. (Young children don't have the same sense of time that we do. Six months is an eternity in the life of a two-or three-year old.) They can make plans for a known and loved person to take care of the first child at the baby's birth time. They can refrain from talking about this new person as a playmate for the older child; it would take eons, in the young person's time framework, for an infant to grow enough to be a possible playmate. They can encourage the older child to help hold the bottle, hold the diapers and powder. They can sensitively help the child to feel a part of the many operations that are so time-consuming around the new baby, without demanding service to the baby when the older child isn't interested. They can brace themselves for such comments as "I hate that baby." You might say, "I can tell that sometimes it's very hard for you when I have to pay so much attention to the baby. Let's plan a special time together. What do you think you might like to do with me without the baby?"

It is vital to always recognize the child's feelings even when you're tired and rushed. Try to do something for the child to help her replace her feelings of anger and abandonment with ones of love and care. Sometimes it's harder for adults than for children to accept the angry feelings young people feel for their younger siblings. Life becomes difficult indeed unless the angry feelings are understood and accepted.

As your children grow up, there will be many times when they enjoy and appreciate each other, and many times when each is the last person the other wants to be with. Some siblings are fast friends for life and some are not.

It's hard on the whole family to absorb a new baby into the family constellation. Some find it easier than others. The way adults handle the situation can make a world of difference. If feelings can be accepted by everyone much of the time, there will be fewer issues of guilt and pain, and more possibility of pleasure in the various relationships.

Children often make up after squabbles and become exceptionally close. They learn not only to handle anger but to express concern and love. They learn this best if it's voluntary, rather than forced by a parent who intrudes too much in their fights.

Parents can support the love children usually have for each other by commenting on it when it is evident. It's always more effective to support positive behavior than to condemn what we consider negative. The experience of working things out with a sibling stands one in good stead in later life.

Let Them Be Their Age

It's wonderful when we can let children be their own age. When we can't, we take something away from them. We succumb to the ads which encourage them to grow up fast. We give them Barbie dolls with breasts and grown-up clothes. We buy them camouflage pants which mimic the army. We're sometimes unwilling to let them enjoy just being children.

"But children clamor for these things!" Aren't they responding to bombardment by advertisers? We have given over some of our judgment about child-rearing to manufacturers and sellers, who entice us to give our child everything. They're skillful (and cynical) in their ability to appeal to the guilt most of us carry. "I'm not doing enough for my child." They convince us that our three year-old needs nail polish. They tell us that our infant will read in minutes if we buy this tape or record, that book or endless series of books. We are sometimes so eager to be good parents that we spend money we can't afford on materials our children can't really use (or, too often, shouldn't use). We want to speed our child's growth, and outpace the Jones's.

Sometimes we as parents fall for the notion that children need all kinds of lessons: gymnastics, ballet, piano, hockey technique, mathematics camp. We dress them up in grown-up outfits for recitals, and take their grandparents to ooh and ah over their cuteness as they pretend to be grown up in their tutus. Many children *do* profit from lessons, gaining skill in the use of their bodies through gymnastics, growing in self-confidence because of development of music ability. Many, though, are pushed into lessons they don't enjoy and which don't enrich their lives.

Unfortunately, we too often tell them "You're too big to cry" when they're hurt, and not to be noisy, not to get dirty, not to be silly.

Hear my plea: let young children be their age. Let them run and climb and jump in the parks and the woods. Let them sing and yell and enjoy their voices and bodies without someone else telling them how to do it. Let's stop buying adult clothes and paraphernalia. Let's not focus on their appearance. Let's concentrate on their joy in living. Let's encourage spontaneity above rehearsed performance.

Young children deserve to live life to the hilt as three-year-olds, as four-year-olds, as five-year-olds. Plenty of time remains for them to be grown up. Spontaneity and creativity are qualities we value in people. Our children already possess them, so let's not eclipse their innate openness to life. Running free, yelling, digging in the dirt, rolling in the grass, laughing hysterically, making absurd faces, building sand castles, wrecking and building them again: such is the fabric of a free, enriched childhood. Children will use their time productively if we stay out of their way. Their inborn desire for growth tells them what will help them become those thoughtful, creative, imaginative, loving human beings we ourselves want to be.

Fears

"There's a tiger under my bed and it's going to eat me!" screams four-year-old Jessica. "There's only empty space under your bed," we reassure her. "Tigers only live in the jungle." We cannot dispel her fears. She knows her fears are real. She may begin to think something is wrong with her if her parents tell her that what she is feeling is not so.

Perhaps you can comfort Jessica. Acknowledge that you know she is scared, and say to her, "Tell me about the tiger." Her answer may help you understand what she is feeling about herself. Most fears are expressions of feelings inside. The tiger might be Jessica herself, for instance, feeling jealous of her baby brother. Her parents have made it clear that they expect her to love him. Sometimes she does, and sometimes she doesn't. What is she to do with her feelings of anger and resentment? Sometimes she'd like to gobble him up so he'll go away forever. Such an idea, she has learned, would be dangerous to express, so in hiding her occasional hatred for her brother (perhaps from both her family and herself), a tiger comes to the surface.

Our children need to be accepted as they are, good and bad, lovable and irritating, generous and selfish. They need reassurance that all parts of them are acceptable, even if all are not welcome. We can tell them that we understand their mixed feelings, and encourage them to express these feelings. We can help them see that talking about their feelings is not the same as acting on them. A child may not hit, but it is all right to tell how angry she is.

When we adults resist our impulse to be logical (when we learn to listen to a child's feelings and not contradict them), then we can nourish their need to grow into people ready to accept the many complexities and opposing forces in themselves.

Sometimes a child is so frightened by her feelings that she cannot talk about them directly. Puppets and dolls can be very useful at such times. The child feels safe talking for a doll, or a furry puppet animal. The adult will learn a little about the child's feelings, and can begin to help the child to accept her contradictory aspects. Parents can tell stories that mirror their children, disguising them enough to make their listeners feel safe, but familiar enough to illustrate what the parent may not want to say outright. Children can decipher sophisticated messages if they are delivered with love, humor and imagination.

Imaginary playmates are often made to be responsible by a child for her own unacceptable behavior, "No, I didn't eat those cookies, but I think Billy Bob did. Billy Bob, you are a bad boy. Let's spank Billy Bob." Henry has already developed a conscience. He knows he shouldn't have taken cookies, but finds it difficult to own up to it, and acknowledge he has done something he shouldn't. Invisible Billy Bob takes the blame. He tries to distance himself from his "bad" self. This is an appropriate way for young children to learn to cope with having a shadow side.

Preschoolers are helped by knowing that all young children have similar fears, knowing that these fears are a part of growing up and part of their imperfect selves. When my granddaughter was four, she often woke up crying, afraid of wolves. I told her that I could understand how afraid she was, and that I would look in my best book on children, *The Infant and the Child in the Culture of Today,* and see if I could learn anything to help her. When I read to her "Many four-year-olds are afraid of wolves," she gave a big sigh of relief, smiled, and wrapped her arms around my neck. I often think of this when I am putting a child to bed.

Part Three

Validation

Jamie was four. In his mother's eyes, he could do nothing well. She was at her wit's end with him, and described him, with sadness and pity, as a total failure. She and I had many conferences, trying to find ways to help him release some of his likable sides. I asked her what he did well; she could think of nothing. In desperation I asked how he brushed his teeth. She replied that he was an expert at tooth-brushing, giving it energy and attention. I proposed that she start from that place, and genuinely affirm him. She thought it a little ridiculous, but agreed to try. When we talked a few days later, I realized that she was liking him a little bit. She said, however, that nothing had changed. I urged her to have faith and continue. As the days passed—since she was now looking on him with a little more favor—she began to see other things she could approve. He always ate everything on his plate, he went to sleep as soon as his head hit the pillow. For the first time in his life, Jamie was hearing appreciative words from his mother. Naturally, he liked this new warmth and love, and wanted more. Gradually he began to change other behavior. His mother liked what she was seeing, and began to refrain from commenting on what she didn't like. It took a long time for major changes to occur, but they did. Jamie's mother had been so unhappy that she was willing to make a large effort to change her responses to him. I kept reinforcing her, as she reported minor improvements and surprises. I felt excitement, and was able to support her in the difficult task of changing herself, and thereby helping her child change. We can only change others as we ourselves change.

When we shift our focus of attention on our young children, verbally acknowledging that we see their successes and their risk-taking, our children are freed, and may thrive. We'll love them more, appreciate them more. We will in fact feel closer to them. What a large gain for such a small investment.

Phil Donahue says in his autobiography, "If I could start parenthood over again—and I wish I could—the biggest change I'd make is in stroking. Out loud. When my kids pleased me, I never told them so. Children get criticized, and pushed and pulled as though they were clay, to be molded (and spanked) into praiseworthy adults reflecting the virtues of their parents."

Sometimes it is hard to believe that young children depend on our approval, particularly when they have been bent on doing everything of which we don't approve. They need our attention desperately, and they'll get it one way or another.

Somehow we've put into our heads that we will spoil children if we let them know how much we are pleased by them. I think there is danger in praising children, saying "You're such a good boy." "You do the most beautiful artwork." "You are the best girl in the world." Praise is subtly but radically different than affirmation. Haim Ginott points out in *Between Parent and Child* that a child may be harboring angry thoughts at the moment she is called 'a good girl,' or feel inadequate or bad. She knows she's not a good girl, and she's confused. She also knows that if adults can praise her, they can also criticize her, so it may not be such a good idea to take many risks.

How, then, do we display our pleasure in our child's actions or work? We can describe what they are doing. We can say, "I saw that you worked very hard and long raking those leaves. Thank you." This is appreciation without judgment. A child can say to herself "My mother loves me," or "I'm a good leaf-raker," or "I am strong." It's her own message to herself, and she knows we appreciate her.

Unconditional Love

How often I wish to be loved and appreciated just for who I am, not for my deeds and accomplishments! I experienced unconditional love from my father in his later years. My parents were divorced when I was eight; I didn't see my father for the next ten years. I felt that I must have done something wrong to cause them to separate. I certainly did not feel loved by my father. As an adult I moved to the same geographic area as my father, and began to have regular contact with him. He grew to know me well, at last, and to appreciate my work. He liked to hear me tell about my days working at school. He always said, when I told him a story about children, "Did you write that down? Sometime you'll be writing a book about your work with children." I didn't believe him, but I enjoyed his obvious approval of me. Gradually I began to notice that he loved me! His love didn't seem tied to what I was accomplishing. It seemed that he loved me just because I was me, just because I exist. I remember feeling that he loved me so much that it wouldn't matter at all if I failed miserably at something; he would continue to love me. What a relief! An enormous burden was lifted from me. I no longer had to perform in order to earn his love. It was simply there, and would be there forever, regardless of what I did. I fervently hope that others can find such resolution with their parents at an earlier age than I did.

What a gift we make when we give unconditional love. We free the recipient from constant doubt. We remove their need to perform in order to receive. We allow them to relax, to take it easy. Our children need our unconditional love. They need to know that we love them regardless of what they do. They can do dumb things, be clumsy, act stupid; they can lie and cheat, they can be furious with us, they can fail at school or anywhere . . . and we will still love them. What a relief to them when this message gets through.

I wonder how many of us feel loved unconditionally. Do we trust that we will be loved even if we do not act and live at our highest level, all the time? Are we afraid of rejection if we are not warm and friendly all the time? If we have a best friend, is it someone who will stand by us however we behave? Is it someone with whom we can be ourselves?

I believe that we all look for unconditional love from our spouses and partners. Perhaps one of the changes from the first enveloping love of courtship is the change from unconditional to conditional love. We feel, during the honeymoon phase of our coming together, that we can do no wrong, we are loved absolutely. Some time after the first blush of love has gone, many of us begin to realize that we are loved for the way we act to our partners, or for the way we dress, and cook, and tell jokes. We feel cheated. We aren't loved unconditionally after all! We've got to perform.

Some of us have found that our relationship to our partner has changed dramatically over time. We begin to trust each other more deeply. We learn to let down our guard, to be our true selves. We discover a myriad of ways to check that the love is indeed still there. We let down more of our guard. A few of us, the lucky ones, discover that we are unconditionally loved, however rotten we may sometimes appear to ourselves. All of our children, indeed, all of the world's children, deserve unconditional love from us. But they do so many unlovable things! How does a father express his love to his daughter when she has reduced her little brother to tears for the fifth time that day? Her dad is frustrated and self-righteous. How did I beget this hideous creature?

Take some deep breaths. Then say something like this: "Kim, I understand that Malcolm drives you crazy by following you around. You want to be left alone. It's hard for you to see how much he admires you and wants to be where you are. You get fed up with him, and hit him and tease him. He thinks you don't love him. I love you both very much. I understand how much he irritates you. You need to find some way of getting privacy, but not by teasing and hitting Malcolm."

Fantasy

THE DIFFERENCE BETWEEN REALITY and FANTASY

"So robbers are real?" Samantha asked after a neighbor's house was burglarized. It's not surprising that children have a hard time telling the difference between what is real and what isn't. They pretend all day long, imagining that their dolls are real, that their trucks are real. They see nature programs on television, in which real animals sleep and roam. They see monsters on television, and people let them know that they're pretend. I once told a four-year-old who was discussing scary monsters, "Monsters aren't real." "I know," she said. "Except for the one under my bed." She was afraid at night, and projected that fear onto the one remaining monster that possibly stalked the land.

We encourage children's fantasy play. We like to see them acting out real-life situations. We think they're learning about the world this way, and yet we are sometimes concerned when a child has an imaginary playmate. We seem to want them to know, at all times, what is pretend and what is real, but they don't have the experience to do it.

I, too, am frightened by the unreal. I never watch scary programs on television because I know that my sleep will be disturbed. I know very well that what I'm seeing is not real, but I too fear the monster under my bed. To best help children make these distinctions, be relaxed about them. Accept an imaginary friend; set an extra place at the table. Your child will be pleased by your acceptance. The only time one need be concerned about imaginary playmates is when a child never plays with real children. Then it's time to look deeper into what's going on in your child's life.

We like to make up bedtime stories for children. They want to know if these are real or pretend. We model creativity and imagination by making things up. Then we may tell a young child that she is lying when she tells something not factual. How confusing life is for young children. Accusing a young child of lying is not useful. Sometimes I say, "You really wish you had a brother, don't you?", if a child is claiming one I know she doesn't have.

We sometimes push children into telling untruths. The last time I did this was many years ago. There was a beautiful flower garden in front of the school. One day a child arrived with a handful of flowers. She held them out joyously, saying "These are for you." I recognized them. Instead of commenting that these flowers are for looking at, not picking, I said, "Thank you. Where did you get these?" There it was: the Trap. The child said "From home," and her mother, in distress, said "From the school garden." I realized that I had caused this untruth. I know better than to ask a question whose answer I already know; it is disrespectful and manipulative.

Caretakers of young children often discover that a child has done something. They ask, "Did you take a cookie from the cookie jar?" They are almost ensuring that the child will slip out of the truth and deny the charge. I have learned that we can either ignore the cookie-taking or come right out with what we know. Hidden agendas cause misunderstandings and power games. Let's not take unfair advantage of our young people.

GRANTING in FANTASY WHAT WE CAN'T in REALITY (or, YES, WE HAVE NO BANANAS)

Children wish for many things. Television advertisements convince them that they must own the latest mechanical toys. Young children feel relatively powerless, and imagine that they'd feel strong if they had lots of possessions. We adults sometimes share this misapprehension.

When children long for things, we may tell them, "No, you can't have that." They whine, fuss, beg; they're again refused. A different scenario might go like this. Andy, age four, has just eaten the last of the bananas. He begs for another. His father knows that there are no more bananas, so he says, "Andy, if I had lots and lots of bananas, how many would you want?" Andy looks surprised and thinks for a minute. "Twenty thirty." His dad gives Andy a big smile and puts his arm around the boy. "Andy, if I had lots and lots of bananas I would give you twenty thirty." Andy looks appreciatively at his father, and runs off to play.

What was happening here? This man was recognizing his child's feelings rather than reasoning with him. It's natural to try to reason with a young child who's unhappy or angry. Andy's father acknowledged Andy's longing by granting in fantasy what he couldn't in reality. Pointing out to Andy that there were no more bananas wouldn't have helped. Andy was aware of it; more importantly, it was his wanting that his father needed to recognize, not the facts. Andy was thrilled that his father understood him so well, and cared so much that he'd do the impossible if he could. This situation might have ended with two angry people. Instead, two people felt more warmly towards each other at that moment.

I learned this technique from the psychologist Haim Ginott. In his book *Between Parent and Child* he elaborates on this theory. He talks about children's constant need for reassurance, as distinct from praise, and for words of love and appreciation. Ginott helped me see how important it is to deal with feelings, rather than ignoring them or trying to reason them away.

Adults want our feelings acknowledged, too. Many of us like to fantasize. Maybe we feel that we're the only ones who don't get to travel to exotic places. If I'm complaining about this and my partner responds, "Honey, if we had all the money in the world, where would you like to go?" I would stop to think for a minute and then I would say, "I'd like to go to every single country in Europe." "If we had all the money in the world, we would go to every single country in Europe, and never come home," he'd say, and I would feel very understood.

Yes-Saying and Expedience

How often do we say 'yes' to our children? When I'm working with young children I sometimes find myself saying 'no' more often than I myself like to hear. I back off for a moment and ask myself what is happening. Why do I need to wield such power? Am I feeling particularly fragile today? Am I tired or sick? My normal way of dealing with children is to say 'yes' as often as I possibly can. I don't want to engage in power struggles with them. I want young people to know that their ideas are worthwhile, and to expect a 'yes' whenever possible. Since they know my usual responses, they don't need to test me by asking outrageous things. They know that I am on their side, that I am there to assist them, and they can trust me.

Why is it sometimes so hard for parents to affirm their children? When we are tired or rushed, it sometimes seems easier to turn down all requests automatically. Saying 'yes' may involve work, or mess, or focusing seriously. In the long run we want to encourage their curiosity, and their desire to learn, and we want them to feel safe sharing their innovative ideas. We want them to be persistent, just not always with us, when we're busy, tired or want to relax.

Your child wants to help cook supper. "Fred," you might say, "I'm just too tired." You know it will take longer, and you'll make a bigger mess. But sometimes you'll find that you can think again. It would give the two of you a chance to do something together, and Fred would be thrilled to help you. Who cares if supper is later than usual? You can let your son know that you appreciate his ideas, that you like to do things with him, and that he can share in the work of the family. What an affirmation of your child!

Since most of the house is designed for adults, it may be difficult for children to work comfortably in the kitchen. Perhaps he can sit on the counter, or on a high stool, or work at a low table. Perhaps you can slow down and remember the pleasure of creating something with your child.

If people often say 'no' to me, at work or elsewhere in my life, I often become discouraged. I'm less ready to be helpful when previous offers of help have been rejected. I'm a resentful employee when my ideas aren't welcomed. I visualize my boss saying, instead, "I like that you are always thinking about ways of making the work more productive. Let's talk more about this idea and see if there are ways we can put it into effect." The more we say 'yes,' the more enthusiasm we generate in others and in ourselves.

I attended a church supper recently. I was seated near a family which included a two-year-old girl. Yang was alert, active and enthusiastic. She loved the chowder. She wouldn't drink it from a cup ("No way!"). She preferred ladling it into her mouth with a spoon. There were no high chairs available, so her mouth was at the level of the table. She managed to slurp about half of the chowder into her mouth. The rest stuck to her face or rolled down her chest. Her mother supported her feeding herself with encouraging words. I didn't once hear the generally pointless comment "Be careful." She was pleased with her independence, and valued it more than she worried about her mess. Her cup was refilled again and again. When she was finished, she slipped off her chair and wandered over to another table to visit her grandmother. Her parents kept their eyes on her, but didn't restrain her subsequent travels around the room, since she was bothering no one. I was struck by the comfortable relationship these young parents maintained with their daughter. They recognized that independence is at the fore in their young girl's life, and they valued it, not thwarted it. What made the biggest impression on me was the lack of the word 'no.'

Some parents would have scolded her for spilling; tried to feed her themselves; disallowed her wandering. When parents curb their children when it's unnecessary, they are invalidating them. The child hears, "I am not O.K." Yang will probably grow up with a strong sense of her own worth, and others will enjoy her as much as I did at the chowder supper.

When it's time for work and his child doesn't have her shoes on, a father can yell at his daughter and hurriedly jam her shoes onto her feet, or he can help her, all the while explaining that on this day they need to leave within a minute, and that tomorrow he will watch her put on her shoes by herself. The latter is a parent who understands that expedience can coexist with his respect for his daughter. Parents and teachers can give children lessons in putting on shoes, snow pants and jackets, in using scissors, in solving conflicts. They can also do the chore themselves when it is necessary, for reasons of safety or time, without taking away the child's independence. I often stop and tell myself. "We are on the same side. I simply have more experience and more power."

Bribery

Most parents resort, from time to time, to bribery. They can't stand the whining and defiant behavior happening between them and their child. How often do you bribe your children? If you find that it is frequent, stop, and try to figure out the reason. Is it because there is so much conflict with your child? Your expectations may be too high, and you may be forgetting to take into account her way of thinking. She doesn't think as you do. Perhaps you've left too little time for things or time has dragged you along, no matter how much you've tried to slow it down. Maybe you need to show your child that you're in charge. Think about what bribes imply.

To bribe is to buy off, to avoid dealing with an issue. It's a way of getting your own way without a power struggle (something we generally try to avoid). It's usually a gesture of helplessness and frustration. Bribes offer material goods or permission for action in order to pacify the other; they constitute an admission that the other has the balance of power at the moment; they represent the ultimate in manipulation.

Some of the above definitions sound harsh. I mean them to, because I so thoroughly disapprove of bribing. I believe that bribery leads to bribery leads to bribery. The avoidance of issues covered by bribing causes untold damage to the relationship between child and parent. The child is cheated because she is robbed of opportunities to work things out with her parent. She misses out on vital development of problem-solving skills. She learns that her parent is weak, not strong. She becomes an expert manipulator herself, because she has learned how easily her parent capitulates and comes up with a reward. Such children resort to whining and pouting, not having developed the usual social skills. They aren't pleasant to be around, and haven't developed the ability to negotiate or to take no for an answer.

How do we stop? I recommend talking with friends about solutions they have developed. When my first child was quite young, I organized a child study-group for this purpose. We met regularly in the evenings. We read books and articles, reporting on them to each other, and occasionally invited speakers. I remember being shocked to learn at one of these meetings that one of the mothers had threatened to cut off her son's penis if he masturbated again! I don't remember if we were able to help her see the numerous reasons for our dismay. How devastating such a threat could be to his future feelings about his body and sexuality, how distrustful he could become of his mother, and how natural and important masturbation is in the psycho-sexual development of children. I am sure that many of the sexual difficulties of today's adults are related to the ways in which their parents reacted to their early exploration of their bodies.

In talking with friends or your partner, you might make a list of situations which result in your resorting to bribes. I'm a great believer in parents discussing behavior they are sorry to discover, either in themselves or in their children. Making lists and writing in diaries can also be useful. We are so close to situations that concern us that we need to devise methods of stepping back to get a more objective look. I begin to see patterns of behavior if I can see them listed over a period of days. I might discover that I always bribe at the end of the day. Am I too tired? Can I build in a few minutes of rest and relaxation before having to deal with my child then? Can I find a few minutes for gazing, fantasizing, deep breathing? Can I re-energize myself to help me get through a trying period with more aplomb?

Perhaps it's my child, not me, who's always tired in the afternoons. There are probably things I can do to relieve *her* tiredness, or prevent it. Let's brainstorm. How about, "Go out for supper every night."? O.K., it isn't practical, but it lets you know where to start. Go to a fast-food restaurant when everyone is exhausted; go another time when everyone feels fine, just for the fun of it. Cook lots of food on Sundays and freeze it; swap a meal a week with neighbors. The important thing is to find the causes of the biggest stresses and work to relieve them.

When stress is lessened, or at least identified, you can think about substitutes for bribing. If you've just picked up your child from school, and you might ordinarily say "I have a surprise for you in the car," say instead "I'm so glad to see you! I was thinking about you when I was having lunch, wondering if you were eating that peanut butter and jelly and mustard sandwich we made together. I loved when we used the cookie cutter on it." Hug her while you talk. The message the child receives is "My dad loves me; he misses me; he likes doing things with me." The parent who too often brings a material surprise is saying, in effect, that he himself is not enough to offer; he must have something to give to his child. Such devices can keep child and parent from being close, and introduce the idea of buying emotions and behavior. The parent offering the surprise does not realize this; he thinks it is a wonderful show of love. In moderation, it can be so. When used too much, it can harm the growing sense of loving each other for being ourselves.

One of the difficult things about bribing is that it becomes habit-forming on both sides. The child wants more and more, and asks you to raise the ante again and again. When the child is given the parent instead, the reality of the gift is so clear and so real that the child feels no need for more.

It's hard to break the bribery habit. It's hard to break any habit. Look at the number of groups and manufacturers involved in trying to help people stop smoking, drinking, overeating and abusing. We all benefit when we help to change habits which work against the self-interests of our young children.

Manners and Integrity

We enjoy a well-mannered child; we often dislike a child who does not seem genuine. How do we get one without the other?

Our children copy us. If we genuinely care for others, our children are likely to develop similar values and behavior. If we say one thing and think another, our children are likely to develop superficial manners without real depth of feeling for other people.

If we require a child to say "I'm sorry" after she has hurt another, we are usually encouraging her to be deceitful. It is unlikely that she is really sorry. She says the words in order to please us, or to escape our displeasure. Most children are not sorry when they have grabbed something, hit someone, said something unpleasant. They act on impulse; they live in the present, doing what occurs to them at that moment. When the event is over, it's over. They do not ruminate and change their minds about having done these things.

So many things are so confusing for young children that it makes me sad when we add to their confusion with our own needs. I want us to raise people of integrity, people who have the courage to say what they believe, and people who will be likely to *feel* sorry if they have hurt another. In order to do this, we can model integrity for them, not urge them into deceit. You may ask, "Isn't this just a tiny lie? Something to make another feel better?" Young children cannot make that kind of distinction. They can only take this as validation for saying what gets them out of a situation most easily. I don't think that is what we really want to be teaching them.

When our child does something we don't like, we can say we are sorry. We can let our child know, and another child, for instance, whom she has hurt, that we don't like that behavior. We can acknowledge her feelings (always an important thing to do). We might say, "I know you were really angry; you wanted that toy and you wanted it right now. It's hard to wait. I'm sorry you hurt your friend. He didn't like that." And then it is important to stop talking. I believe we all go on much too long when we are disappointed in our children. Then we wonder why they don't listen. They've often heard more than they want to hear, so they turn us off. What an effective mechanism that is!

If we tell children to say "thank you" to another person, in an attempt to teach manners, we are treating the child like a puppet. We often embarrass her by telling her to do something while we are standing right in front of someone else. She is likely to shrink to our side, drop her head and become acutely uncomfortable. How much better if we say "thank you" for her. Later we can discuss with her how people like to be thanked, and how we know she will learn to do this as she begins to notice people thanking each other, or her. Letting our child know that we believe in her is a powerful tool.

We probably direct our children in their behavior in front of others in order to appear to be concerned and responsible parents. We want others to see us as parents who know what is right, and who are putting our children through their paces. In time we may realize that we care even more about the children than about what others think of us.

Sexual Abuse

Ricardo is with his favorite baby sitter, Michael, who is fourteen. Ricardo goes to the toilet and Michael follows. Michael watches Ricardo urinating. Then Michael says, "My penis is much bigger than yours. Do you want to see it?" There follows a time of comparing and touching. This is highly inappropriate behavior on Michael's part, and should be stopped. It is sexual abuse, in that Michael is using his position as an older person, and a person temporarily in charge of Ricardo, to expose his genitals to the younger boy, and to touch Ricardo's genitals.

What can be done in such a situation? If Ricardo, age five, has talked about the subject of sexuality and sexual abuse, and perhaps participated in some discussions in his school or day care center, he may be able to tell his parents about this experience, and they can talk to Michael. It is unlikely that they will decide to continue hiring him. (I would consider letting Michael continue to babysit only if several things were to happen: if the parents felt, after serious talks with Michael, that he understood and agreed with their beliefs, if Michael's own parents or guardians were involved in the talks, and if all of us felt strongly that this behavior was genuinely changed, and that the various relationships among the two families were strong and ongoing.)

How can we talk with young children about abuse without frightening them unduly? Why take the chance of traumatizing them unnecessarily? The facts are these: one recent study shows that from a third to a half of all children in the U.S are sexually assaulted or abused in some way before they turn eighteen. And who does this to them? In the majority of cases it is a person they know, often a relative or friend of the family. And are these isolated incidents, generally happening only once to a particular child? No, they are much more likely to be repeated, sometimes happening over many years. Are these violent attacks? No, often they are subtle, with the perpetrator unfairly insinuating herself or himself into the confidence of the child.

It is no longer enough to warn children about strangers. They need to thoroughly understand four things: that their bodies are private; that it is *always* all right to tell adults "no" when it comes to the touching of bodies or of going somewhere with anyone they don't know; that they *must* tell trusted adults if anyone touches their bodies or talks of touching them in ways that make the children uncomfortable; and that it is *not* their fault if someone does so.

How does one tell children such things? Gradually and frequently. If you enjoy telling stories to your children, this is a good vehicle for suggesting ways to deal with these situations. You can make up a story about a child your child's age, or even tell a made-up story about the child herself, and describe some of the situations that might occur. Make the child in the story gradually work out ways of dealing with the intruding people. The child in the story may not know right away what to do, but begins to figure things out. This technique will probably cause discussion with your child. You can discuss the story solutions, and ask her what she thinks about them.

Discuss the fact that we all have the right to decide who touches our bodies. Give examples of parts of the body someone might want to touch, and then say, "You can tell this person "no," or you can run away." It is important for a child to know that she can come to you and tell you if any person touches her in a way that does not feel good, and that even though the perpetrator may have said "Don't tell anyone!" the child should always tell you, or a teacher, or another adult the child considers safe and reliable.

It is vital to make very clear to children that if a person exposes himself or herself to her, or touches private parts of her body, it is not her fault. She needs to be reassured that you will help her, and not blame her, regardless of whether you think she should have known better, and regardless of how she handled it or took part in it. She needs to trust that you are with her all the way, in helping her work through the experience and helping her develop more adequate defenses in case she meets a similar situation.

Forewarned is forearmed. Adults and older children are powerful people to young children, and they're often in a position to harm them. You can offer help, encouragement and good ideas ahead of time. Help your child feel strong enough and knowledgeable enough to deal with such difficult situations when you're not around.

War Toys

Two four-year-olds run, chase, brandish toy guns, shoot each other. They shout, "I got you"…"you're dead"…"I got you again"…I shot you in the head." Later in the day they play with toy cars and trucks. Martine grabs a truck from Willy. Willy punches her in the head. Martine punches back. Both end up in tears, mad at each other.

Is there any connection between the play of these children at two different activities? I think so. Playing with violent toys breeds violence. We shouldn't be surprised. We practice skills in order to become better at them. We believe that nurturing one's dolls is practice for becoming nurturing parents. We believe that playing cooperative games teaches cooperative attitudes. So it should not surprise us that gun play fosters violence.

Our warlike government, in order to dehumanize our enemies (and promote the violence needed for war) has shown Germans, Japanese, Vietnamese, Iraqis as rats, spiders, vile creatures to be smashed to oblivion.

Dorothy P. Lindorff, child therapist, says (of the Rambo doll), "He kills hundreds of people violently, like a machine, without feeling. He can only be thought of as an evil force. A hero should be an example of hope, strength and life. Not war, power, killing and death."

In choosing toys for your children it can be useful to think about what kind of people you want them to become. If you want your children to become aggressive and violent, you choose toys that encourage such play. If you want them to become cooperative, curious, friendly and concerned with the well-being of others, choose toys that give them a chance to practice those skills.

Dr. Charles Turner, Ph.D., University of Utah, suggests: "Playing with violent toys increases the risks that children are going to use aggression in real life at a later time. The violent toys serve as a way of rehearsing the violent behavior seen on television. They increase the likelihood that the effects of cartoon violence will carry over to the playground and into their everyday life."

The people cited above are but two of many who take the position that playing violently and watching violence on television increase violence. We need to make some hard choices. If we decide to take a stand on this issue with our children, we will have to struggle against the tide of those who take a more relaxed attitude about war play. We have to make clear to our children our moral position about war and violence. We will have to help them understand why they are not allowed to play with toy guns and military action figures or watch violent cartoons on TV. If you don't believe that most cartoons are violent, watch a few on television. Note the number of times persons and animals are smashed flat against a wall, kicked high in the air, exploded by dynamite, pushed off cliffs, punched and battered so that they break into a thousand pieces. That's violence.

Materialism

We live in a society and at a time when it is difficult for us to resist materials. Everything shouts at us to buy, buy, buy. Our children get the message from television constantly; there are more toy stores then ever before; there are toys in the grocery and the drug store. Madison Avenue screams to us that we must constantly buy our children things in order to be good parents. On every front, parents are bombarded to join the materialistic parade. How can we resist? How can we even think that it might be appropriate to resist?

Many parents struggle to make ends meet, even when the household produces two incomes. Two salaries seem to be not quite enough. Child-care costs seem to take most of one salary. Rent or mortgage, food, clothing, insurance, and a few odds and ends seem to take the rest. Wouldn't it be a relief to get off the buying bandwagon? It would relieve the pocketbook and would have a salubrious effect on the children, though neither would necessarily show immediately. It takes a while to give up any addiction, and buying is an addiction for many parents and children. Bruno Bettelheim says that shopping is the only activity that most parents and children do together with any regularity. How sad. Let's see if we can replace it with things more likely to have long-term beneficial effects on children.

Young children are curious and creative by nature. They like to investigate, take apart, put together and figure out new combinations. Many of today's toys do not cater to those interests. They are either part of a series of dolls or creatures (Barbie dolls, Ninja Turtles, G.I. Joes), part of a series of motor vehicles (elaborate mechanized toys that require little of the child), or dollhouses, barns and garages that replicate the real thing. Few of these toys call for imagination on the part of the child. Too much is supplied by the manufacturer. Today's toys are so specific that it is less easy to turn them into something else than it used to be. When toys were more generic ("a doll," "a car"), they were more likely to be transformed into many different cars and dolls by the imagination of the child. Today's child has to have many more toys because that adaptability is no longer so available.

The creative impulses in children need nurturing. A friend says, "One of the best birthday party activities we ever had for one of our sons (age about ten) was a hammer, a board, and lots of nails. Both our boys spent hours happily and noisily hammering nails, in obvious delight. The best presents I ever gave my nieces and nephews: a canteen, a length of clothesline, a spool (about eighteen inches high and twenty-four inches in diameter, salvaged from an electrical store, and which I painted a bright color), and a home-sewn, reversible cape (different colors on each side) with ties to go around the neck."

A child can put her creativity into practice more easily if she has fewer toys, and less specific ones. Some children are so surfeited with toys that it is difficult to make selections for play. Let's imagine for a minute that all your children's toys are destroyed in a fire. You want to help them start building up their collection all over again. Make a list of all of the kinds of toys your child played with most often (kinds, not specific brands). If your child is a Barbie-doll addict, this is the time to wean her. Then go to several stores and buy the most generic, non-specific examples of the things on your list. Maybe you'll return with a doll that could be either gender (not so easy to find), dolls representing different racial groups, a truck, a car, a ball. You and your child can start looking around the house to see what you can add from things you already have. Think about empty cans (with rough edges smoothed), pieces of cloth, string, tape, scrap paper and pencils, buttons of different colors and sizes, needles and thread, nails and a hammer, pieces of wood. The list is endless.

Since your child's creativity has likely been dulled by pre-formed toys, it may take some time for her to start exploring the raw materials you have presented. On the other hand, you may be surprised at the speed with which she jumps in. Think how much exploration and individual discovery can go on at the beach, where a child may have only sand, a pail and a shovel. Her creativity was always there; it has simply been covered by the glow of the stereotypical toys offered. Your child will likely throw herself into play when she herself is the creator. She will probably stay longer at play, feel more satisfaction, and develop more sense of herself as a competent person who knows how to do things, and who can invent and discover. She may more often come to ask you to see what she has done or made.

It may be that a fire will not come your way. How will you solve this problem? I know some parents who routinely weed out their children's toys so that they are not so overwhelmed. (I would, in most cases, get your child's permission.) Some talk with relatives and friends beforehand when a birthday is coming, and make sure what's given seems right. Recently I went to a meeting devoted to the subject of children and materialism. Some felt that there was nothing they could do; the situation had gotten out of hand. These were parents who were specifically looking for a simpler life, and yet they were overwhelmed. Others declared that they would start the culling process and eliminate some of their children's toys. Some said they would encourage their children to let go of what they didn't really want or need, with an eye towards giving them to poorer children. This group of parents thought their children might themselves like to take the toys to a center where they were being collected. This idea interests me, and I believe these parents can start discussing the whole idea of possessions with their children. Most young children don't realize that there are many children without such a number of toys. Young people are egocentric and see the world from their own points of view. For the most part they believe everyone is much like them, that they think the same and possess approximately the same. Children find it difficult to imagine otherwise, and are conceptually unable to step out of their own experience. The noted psychologist Piaget says that this phase lasts for a long time, and by around age seven children can *begin* to imagine another's point of view, or another's predicament. Young children may not really understand the concept of scarcity and poverty if it is not an aspect of their lives, but it is always useful to be exposed to ideas we don't understand. The information stays in our brains, where our understanding catches up with the information.

What else can we do? We can take a look at our own buying habits, and at the values we send along to our children. (This is subversive stuff; if we all cut down substantially on our buying patterns, our social system will certainly change.) If we find that we, too, have been caught in the materialism trap, we wonder less how our children have also been caught. Can we change our behavior? Modeling is the best method of teaching. Your children want to be like you. You are the most important person in their lives, and therefore the most powerful influence on them. You might decide to give each other experiences as celebrations, instead of things. You might plan family excursions at birthday times. Perhaps the family together can make a list of trips and activities they would like to do. When a birthday is coming, the honored one could choose from this list. Several things are accomplished by such a plan. Materialism decreases, and children have to depend more on their own resources. The family shares more fun, education, and culture together, and family time gradually changes from shopping to the pursuit of adventure.

Having fewer possessions definitely calls on the creative abilities of a child. There will be more interest in combining, fashioning, constructing. Blocks may emerge as a strong interest. Blocks call on the child to use information she has about the world, particularly unit blocks, based on a system where all sizes are multiples of the smallest. Initially she piles blocks, first constructing large, horizontal structures.

Then she moves to vertical constructions. After a lot of piling variations, she begins to create something from her own experience. It might be houses, farms, stores, fire stations. She will add materials to these buildings as they are available. People are one of the first things she'll probably use, or represent, and then will come vehicles, animals, trees and roads. Blocks make unique creations; no one else has ever built one just like it. It's a true representation of the child, and a lot of herself is in that building.

I've said frequently that my favorite kinds of equipment for young children are blocks, generic dolls, sand, water, clay, paper, scissors and paint. With these, plus scrap materials lying around the house, I believe a young person experiences a rich childhood. With each, she can create. In many cases a child is creating what she knows; in others she is indulging in pure fantasy, playing with ideas based on the merest bits of things she has seen or heard. All of these open-ended toys give free rein to the imagination. Stereotypes are less likely to be introduced. A child gains a sense of her own power, since she is the creator of the combinations, she is the manipulator of the objects, she is the being which breathes life into them. She cannot fail, since there are no standards implicit in the materials. Imagine working in a situation where success is the only possible outcome. Wouldn't you thrive in this environment? Your child will, too, if you are strong enough to take some of the steps I've mentioned, or invent your own. If I have jogged your mind so that you move in this direction, I will have been successful.

Eating

Eating problems happen when caretakers are concerned that their child is not getting enough to eat. The child senses that this is a perfect time to seize power by not cooperating. Not only do power struggles become the mealtime occupation, but the child gets the idea that food is something with lots of emotion invested in it. It's no longer simply growing material and energy for the body. I don't eat when I'm hungry, but when Dad says it's time. One doesn't determine for oneself the amount; that is decided by another. I can discern the roots of eating problems that can last into adulthood. How many of us usually eat because we are hungry? We often use food as a reward, both for ourselves and the people around us. No child starves herself if there is sufficient good food available. Children have periods of fast growth and big appetite, and at other times can exist on very little food. Parents (who may have a hard time separating this new being from themselves in some ways) need to recognize that their appetite and their child's are distinct, and separate.

One of the easiest and most successful methods of dealing with eating problems is the following: measure out teaspoons of each food and put them on the child's plate, making sure to separate the foods so that they don't touch each other. (This is very important to some children.) Then say not a word about eating. If you have, up to this point, been coaxing the eating of most mouthfuls, this approach will be quite a shock to your child. She will be accustomed to getting lots of attention around food, and will suddenly be getting almost none. If she eats the small amount she was served, you might ask her if she wants more of anything, again giving her a measured teaspoon of whatever she wants.

Under no circumstances praise your child for eating. Praise encourages your child to eat for you, not as a result of hunger. If the child eats none or very little, quietly remove the plate and make no comment.

When your young child wants to eat something before the next meal, your response can be a calm, quiet "You can have something to eat at dinner (or whatever is the next meal)." Unless you are able to stick with this program, not worrying that you're starving your child, you'll probably find yourself mired in the power struggles common with eating. You can say, "I can tell that you're hungry" (acknowledging the child's feelings), and "I'm glad that lunch is coming soon." Recognizing feelings helps the child know that you understand how it is for her. Saying "Next time I bet you'll eat when it's on your plate" is not acknowledging feelings, but rubbing in your disapproval and righteousness. Saying things like this may even cause a child to hold out even longer. Your attitude needs to be both casual and genuinely sympathetic. Remember that your child will not starve; that you have a pattern of behavior to change; that it takes time to change established habits. It may be important during this period to serve foods that you know are particular favorites. It is certainly not the time to introduce new foods.

Tell yourself what a good parent you are being, that you are thinking of the long run, not the short. You're helping your child take charge of her eating. You're taking the possibilities of struggling for power out of mealtimes. You are helping your child see that eating can be pleasurable in and of itself. Though it may not seem apparent at first, you are teaching her to eat when she is hungry.

We tend to think that children will be hungry at the times we ourselves are used to eating; it isn't always true. You'll want to watch your child to see what times she appears most hungry, and consider serving the largest meals then. The hours may differ from the ones which guide your own eating. If you've been in the habit of serving a late supper, it's possible that your child has been losing the edge of her appetite by the time you serve food. Someone may have offered a snack too near to the meal. Consider the possibility that children might eat before the adults. Some parents might feel strongly that they want to eat together as a family, and that it can be such a lovely family time. But if, in your experience, the time is not entirely lovely, remember that your children want the attention of their parents, while you are perhaps eager to share news of your day with each other. The adults are often tired; it can turn out to be a time of angry voices, of children being sent from the table, and of general frustration. Think about whether supper time is really the happy time you would like it to be at your house. If it is, keep it up, and congratulate yourself on your ability to parent. If not, consider other alternatives. The eating of food can be a relaxed, enjoyable and truly nurturing experience.

Dressing

Children are very likely to choose the activity of dressing as a place to express themselves. They realize that it is often a hot topic with their parents, and is thus a good time to take a stand and begin to assert their own identities. They may refuse to wear the clothing proposed by their parents, for instance, or refuse to dress at all.

You can help lessen the intensity of the dressing routine by helping your child choose clothes the night before, and by laying them out, ready to be put on in the morning. As an alternative, you might leave several outfits on a chair, so that she can exercise her ability to choose in the morning. She can then feel some power, which is satisfying. Children are struggling for power much of the time.

When should a child get dressed? It often becomes a battleground. Parents are likely to be in a hurry to get the day started. Children's pace is different from adults, as is their sense of the relative importance of things. A child may think that finishing a Lego construction is much more significant than dressing for school. And the more an adult pushes, the more a child is likely to dig in.

Sometimes it makes sense for the parent to dress the child, even though the child is perfectly capable of doing so. This is one solution to eliminating stress and diffusing the battle energy. Many parents have trouble doing this, knowing as they do that the child is able to do it alone. My answer is that it sometimes makes sense to do what expedites things for everyone, without having to worry about the actual capabilities of the child.

The child may be old enough to make an agreement with the parent: "I can work with my Legos as soon as I am dressed." The parent may have to be present to see that this happens. Children can usually dress themselves with great speed if they are motivated to do so.

Clothing should not be too difficult to put on. Buttons on shoulders and in the back are extremely hard. Buckles are not easy for most young fingers. Clear labels marking front and back are helpful in some instances. Until a child can recognize left and right shoes, you can make marks on the inside of each shoe, and she can easily learn to put the shoes together so that the two marks touch.

When a child is first learning to dress, a parent can help a little, watch a little, help some more, watch some more. During this time, give some encouraging words. "Yes, you're certainly learning how to do this. You almost have it. There, it's almost on." A running commentary helps the child feel a sense of accomplishment.

You can give physical assistance at the difficult places and then let the child continue. This gives the child the opportunity to do parts of the job, and to begin gaining a sense of self-competence, surely an attitude important to cultivate. There is a drive in all children to grow and to master skills. It's sometimes thwarted when parents' expectations are not high enough, and when they do too much for their children.

We can constantly assess our child's abilities, and help them move in small steps. It is just as damaging, however, if the expectations are *too* high. Then a child is frequently failing, and may give up trying, because frequent failure hurts. None of us likes to fail; it isn't a useful tool for learning, except in selected doses and very specific times.

Through the daily process of learning to dress, we can help our child develop feelings of competence by trying to become aware of what kind of help she needs from us at any given moment. It may seem to take time we don't have. (How many times have I mentioned this concept in this book?) But, as always: remember the payoff. Soon she can do it all by herself. Her sense of her own abilities is certain to carry over to other areas in which she has been dependent. Her pride and pleasure will carry you over when she is less able to do other things.

Family Meetings

Family meetings are a chance for the whole household to meet on a somewhat equal basis. It's important for the adults to realize that such a meeting is not a good time to foist their decisions on the other members of the family group. It is a time when all have the same opportunity to be heard. I still remember when our youngest child was in charge of a family meeting (we rotated the chair of the meeting). She started the meeting by saying "Will the meeting please come to its orders?" She was beginning to learn, in her individual way, some of the routines of running a meeting. We still have, among our prize possessions, the minutes of some of those meetings. The job of taking the minutes also rotated, except to those who had not yet learned to write.

What are some subjects that might be taken up at family meetings? At the start of meetings, I've found that an open period works, when each is free to tell "goods" and "bads," or what has been going well and what hasn't. This gives each person something to say at the beginning, which sets the stage for equality. There may be a sheet of paper permanently posted where all can suggest agenda items, young ones dictating to an older person. The chair can call for each item to be presented by the one who suggested it. To keep factionalism to a minimum, it is useful to ask each person to first consider what they can support about the proposal, because jumping in immediately to fight an idea makes for less likelihood of open-minded discussion.

Family meetings accomplish many things. They give all the members practice in listening to others. They contribute to a feeling of family unity. Children who participate in family meetings feel more powerful, and recognize that others hear them and take them seriously. Everybody gets some practice in the difficult art of compromise, particularly when parents wield their power gently and thoughtfully. Children gain a sense of themselves as people who have important opinions that others want to hear.

The family almost certainly will have to delegate certain powers to the parents. There may be certain issues where the meetings will not be able to come to consensus. Each family needs to list for themselves issues that are decided by the parents alone, though such a list will probably change over time. Even with the reality of uneven distribution of power, the family meeting can provide a forum for expressing ideas, and an opportunity to try to influence the decision-makers. It should be clear at the outset which areas are open for discussion and change, and which are not. There is nothing more frustrating than discussing something at length, only to discover that under no circumstances will the original decision be changed. That, of course, further underlines the powerlessness of some members; that isn't what we are meeting for. Some businesses operate this way; under cover of a pretense of equality, workers strive to make changes but are, in the end, rebuffed. Morale is not high in these workplaces.

Open communication helps the workings of a family. Children need to be genuinely heard. Parents need to open their minds, relax, and let their children speak their minds, trusting that their parents will take them seriously. Accusations are not in order, but people are encouraged and expected to express feelings about the other family members.

At one family meeting, Jane, a mother, felt extremely upset about the books and clothing strewn so thoughtlessly around the house. When she brought it up at the meeting, she acknowledged that this was primarily her own problem, since she didn't really approve of her own disapproval. Still, she said, it was a serious problem; it distressed her to come home from work to what she considered chaos. The children spent a long time considering a solution to this problem. They finally came up with the idea of a "Disappearing Box." Anyone who found another person's possessions in the common areas of the apartment could put them in this box. There the things would have to stay, dated by a label, for one week. As so often happens, children's solutions are more stringent than parents'. Jane said that it was hard for her not to interfere when it was a real hardship on the owner of things in the box, but she was able to let the ruling stand. Once, one of her sons had to wear bedroom slippers to school because his shoes were in the box. Jane had not been aware that she, too, left things around. The only things that she had noticed lying around belonged to others. One week she left both pairs of dress shoes in the living room. They were promptly incarcerated by one of the children (gleefully, I expect), and Jane was forced to wear sneakers to work until her shoes were released. She told me that all the members of the family began to be much more careful about leaving things around, and began to notice when general cleaning was needed, as well. By announcing at the outset that her frustration was caused by herself, rather than accusing others of being thoughtless or sloppy, she had made it comfortable for the group to come up with a solution. No one had to spend energy defending themselves, since they were not charged with anything.

What are some topics that might be on the agenda for a family meeting? Here are some possible items:

Where to go on family vacations
Meals—what kind of food?
Chores
Particularly annoying situations (smelly cat boxes, junk left around, someone's bed has been outgrown)
Allowances
Room cleanliness
Guests
Noise

Bedtimes
Baths and bathroom use
World affairs
Local affairs
Why it's hard to be a child
Why it's hard to be a parent
Ageism—what is appropriate age for what activity?

Some of these topics relate to the specific family and some are discussions about general issues. It might be interesting for you to make such a list. When families start having family meetings on a regular basis, the agendas are easily filled. There are always items someone wants to discuss.

Each family will have to decide how long the meetings should be, taking special note of the relative attention spans of the young children present. Each family will have to decide about the frequency of meetings. To me, regularity is of great importance, and is far better than holding only emergency sessions, though the latter may be employed as needed. Families begin looking forward to the opportunity to meet and discuss, particularly when they can trust there won't always be big arguments. It's a delightful enjoyment to experience, as a family group, the satisfaction created by having worked through the biggest impediments to unity and pleasure in each other.

I heard a woman tell how meetings were important in her family. She told me that they were especially helpful for her three boys when she remarried. One of the boys, Karl, was particularly suspicious of her new husband, and felt very afraid to try to get close to him. In their meetings, each person started by saying how he or she was feeling about every other member of the family. One day, Karl began the meeting. He said that he was angry at his brother Sven for taking his book and not returning it; he wished his brother Norman would be quieter at bedtime; he didn't like it that his mom had yelled at him about always being late to meals. When he came to his stepfather, he simply said that he was glad to have him in the family.

When it was his stepfather Lee's turn to speak, he said that he refused to accept Karl's statement about his welcome. He felt that Karl had been genuine with the others and not with him. He wanted to hear how Karl really felt about him. At that point Karl broke down, cried, and told Lee that he was afraid to begin trying to accept him and to love him. He had loved his father, and his father had left. He didn't dare reach out to his stepfather, or he, too, might leave. Lee hugged Karl, saying that he truly loved him. He told the boy that he could not guarantee that he would be in the family forever, but that it was his goal; he told him that he *could* guarantee that he would always love Karl. From then on, Karl felt much closer to his stepfather, and began to believe the love coming to him from Lee. He could begin to express all of his feelings, including his fear and anger.

The tradition of family meetings paid off significantly for this family. The boys had learned how to share their feelings long before the stepfather joined them. They had learned, for the most part, to trust each other with their feelings. How lucky they were to receive into their household such an honest and sensitive new member.

Part Four

Creativity

RISK-TAKING

Our society needs people who are willing to take risks; to express wild ideas; to trust their intuition. Our school systems, by and large, do everything they can to stifle that willingness. I talked with a high-school student who volunteers in our school. She verified my hunch; she says that she only dares to raise her hand when she is absolutely sure of the answer. She says she does not dare to question, or to wonder about the absoluteness of answers. The task in her school is to feed back to the teacher what has come from the mouth of the teacher. There is no opportunity to play with ideas, or, therefore, to be creative.

I believe that parents can do a lot to encourage risk-taking in their children. Telling a child to be careful does not protect her; it may, in fact, discourage experimentation and adventure. Parents can support their young children in their reaching out, both in physical ways and in the realm of thinking. Encourage being fanciful, encourage imagination.

When we read stories in our school, we often stop and ask children how they think the people in the story will solve a problem as it arises. We encourage all answers. When I'm reading, I restate what each child says, giving it no more or less weight than the next. We calmly accept doubt about the realism of the story, or dislike of the characters or the action. When we discover how the author solves the problem, we treat that as one of the many possible solutions, not necessarily one that is right. We discuss the fact that this is the way he or she chose, but that he or she might have taken a different path. As a side effect, this approach humanizes authors. Children don't really understand that it is people who write and illustrate books. We always read the names of the author and illustrator before reading a book, to further this understanding.

We play a game at our school with objects hidden in small bags. The children feel the objects through the cloth, and describe what they feel. They might name the actual objects, or they might list some characteristics they discern. Some young children find this easy, for some it's difficult. I suspect that part of the difficulty is the fear of dealing with the unknown, the fear of hazarding a guess when there is little to guide one. The children for whom it is easier feel free to experiment with ideas. They can say "One end is sharp; it's smooth; one part of it can move." We don't tell them they're right or wrong. We talk about fingers being able to feel many kind of textures and shapes, and that sometimes we suddenly realize what something is when we get one more tiny clue.

'Right' and 'wrong' are words I use less and less. Keeping them out of my vocabulary keeps me vigilant. If we use those words often, children develop a pattern of trying to get right answers rather than using their minds. I feel badly when I see the habit of spitting back information inculcated so early in their lives. I like to say things like "I didn't think of looking at this problem as you just did. That's very different than what happened to the girl in the book," and "You're thinking very hard about this."

COOPERATION

Young children are constantly setting problems for themselves. They want to know; they're seekers of truth and knowledge. Many of their efforts at learning are in direct conflict with the adults in their lives. They take things apart that they can't put back together. They make messes. If your young children have tried cooking without your direct supervision, you've seen how engrossed they are in their work. You have also noticed that they don't have the hand control to pour flour directly into the bowl, or to measure a cup of milk without it overflowing to the floor. There is usually a large mess after children work in the kitchen, or the bathroom, or the workshop.

Children are noisy as they experiment with materials. They like to hear the sound of two blocks crashing together, over and over again. They may sing loudly while they work. Non-regimented learning often involves clutter and noise. Children try things out, and learn what happens when they do something a certain way. They do experiments; they're scientists. Competition is not required as a motivator. What's needed are opportunity and reassurance. Adults can extend their interest by occasionally giving new props and materials, but experimentation comes from the child.

I've seen two young children play with a few sticks and stones and some earth. The sticks come alive. They are people, animals, magic wands, helicopters, screwdrivers, giraffe's fingernails. The stones are barns, buses, packages, rhinoceroses. After a time they find a can for water, and add it to the earth. Imagination is constantly at play, and at work. I don't see boredom creeping in, and I don't see competition. They're involved in cooperative, dramatic play, and they are acting out things that are a part of their lives and a part of their fantasies. If one of the children has recently been to a doctor, one of the sticks may be used to give shots, and if one of the children wasn't allowed to go to the circus, the hippopotamuses may trample whatever represents the grown-ups. Dramatic play is vital. Children engage in it as a way of understanding life. They practice. They try out roles in order to integrate their experiences. Young people like to play powerful roles like police, firefighters, doctors or robbers because they generally feel so little power themselves. For a time they become strong; they are in charge.

Playing organized games is usually difficult for young children. It's hard for them to understand the concept of rules, and it's hard to follow rules even when they're understood. Losing at organized games is uncomfortable. They don't see why they have to leave a game of musical chairs simply because they couldn't find a chair to sit in. It doesn't make sense to them.

Cooperative games eliminate the factor of losing and winning. They're played for sheer fun. Many traditional games are easily modified. Musical chairs can be changed so that everyone helps each other find a place to sit, using laps when there are no chairs. The game ends with one chair left, and everyone sitting on the lap of another. There is much hilarity about trying to help each other. A child will call "Here, come sit on my lap," and the pile-ups appeal to their sense of the ridiculous.

In a game called The Wind Blows, children sit in chairs in a large circle. There are a few more chairs than children. The leader says, "The wind blows for people who like peanut butter." All who like peanut butter, generally everyone, move to a new chair. The next call might be "The wind blows for people who have a brother," or "The wind blows for people wearing sweaters," or "The wind blows for people who are laughing." The players sort themselves continuously, in ways that are obvious, complicated, funny. Children eventually take over the leading, and leadership can move around the circle. In such a game, young children have to think about themselves, their likes, their family position, their abilities. It helps them see similarities and differences among the members of the circle. And no one loses.

FOSTERING CREATIVITY

The most valuable materials I see around me in the school are blocks, clay, paints, sand, water, paper and scissors. The less information the material gives its user, the more it fosters creativity. These things can be used successfully by people of all ages, and with each use an original product is made. Success is judged by the creator, since no external standard exists, and failure is virtually impossible. A person feels a sense of power when using these materials; a little effort makes a big change: a flat landscape is quickly changed into a mountain; a square piece of paper becomes lots of triangles; a rectangular compact piece of clay a tremendously long snake.

Our role as adults is to provide children with raw materials, a safe environment and reassurance, and then to back off. Children do not need models imposed by grown-ups. Imagine taking an art course, struggling to draw a tree. The teacher appears and draws a perfect tree on your paper. Rather than encouraging you to look at trees, think about trees, sketch lots of trees in all different ways, the authority has provided you with a model to copy. For the novice artist, that's the moment at which the courage and creative juices dry. That's how children feel when an adult makes a model, or describes something in such detail that it can't be reproduced. Even when the child tries, she can't match it. Rather than making models, adults can show children interest and appreciation. Children feel successful if an adult looks at their work carefully and describes it to them. "That building has a lot of angles in it, and a lot of tall parts." Parents often discover, when they describe a child's work to her, that she can better notice and appreciate details of her own work. I once heard a teacher comment to a four-year-old, "I notice that you used a lot of blue in the corner of your painting, and you stretched out the yellow clear across the page." The child absolutely beamed. "You really noticed! Miss Brown just says 'Oh, that's pretty!'" There's a great difference between praise and attention, and this child responded to it. Children come to depend on praise if we praise them; we prefer that they become critical judges of their own work, deciding for themselves whether and how they like it. When children are praised they become less secure about their own judgment of their products and processes.

What matters is what happens to the child while she's working. The thing she makes today doesn't last; the quality and method of thinking will stay with her.

Observe a young child working with plastic tubing and water, and the difference will become clear. Here's a child standing at a high-sided tray filled with water. She wears a waterproof smock and her sleeves are rolled up. Tubes float in the water. The child moves her hands around in the water, splashing and making waves. She moves a long, transparent tube through the water, and a little bit of water gets into the tube. She sees the bubbles, picks up the tube, and the water spills out. "I can't get any water in this." A teacher moves over to her and remarks, "I wonder how you can do that," remaining near for a while and occasionally commenting on methods the child tries. She swishes the tube more violently in the water, and it fills up more than before. "You're figuring it out." After some time, the child looks in the bin attached to the tray and finds funnels, cups and corks. She investigates each of these in combination with the tubes. After half an hour of independent exploration, she calls the teacher to see that she has solved the problem she set for herself.

Competition

Last Christmas I played with a five-year-old boy for an hour or two. I knew him only slightly, so we got acquainted as we played. He first chose a simple board game he had played just once. We each chose a character to move about the board. A bag held the chips which determined our moves; the chips were various colors and bore various labels. I quickly learned that John interpreted the chips in ways that served our purposes best. If I drew a red chip, which carried the words "Lose Turn," he suggested I draw again, and I certainly found this more fun than losing a turn. As we progressed, each moving one or two steps at a time, I commented that I liked it when we both occupied the same space on the board. John was so taken with this togetherness that he arranged it so that we continued in this fashion, space by space, until we both entered home base at the same moment. We both won! I was charmed that he had chosen to keep us together rather than making sure that he won. It's true that he won the next game, but he saw that I won the third. John was able to be generous and non-competitive because he was totally in charge. He could interpret the rules in any way he chose, and whether he realized or not that we weren't playing as the game maker had intended, he didn't seem to worry about the outcome. Rules being unbreakable was not a concept to which he subscribed.

As I reflected on our games, and John's generosity, it was clear that he enjoyed our being together without my exerting adult power. I think this experience is unusual for a young child. Adults almost always have a large say in play. I had none; he was in charge. He could, then, enjoy our playing, free of competition. Children feel so small and powerless so much of the time that they constantly have to grab and fight for power. When we find ways to empower children, they don't need to struggle for it.

I encourage children to help each other. Competition discourages this, since the emphasis is on bettering another. I affirm children for helping others, letting them know that such gestures are appreciated. When a child spills lots of puzzle pieces, I put out a general call for help. Soon it becomes automatic, and when a child is in evident trouble, others come routinely to help, without being asked. I always appreciate them out loud. Appreciation is effective in continuing a positive behavior. It's nearly impossible to use appreciation too much. When we learn to affirm, there's less need for young children to exhibit what we think of as negative behavior. The positive replaces the negative because of the obvious approval of the adult. All children want attention and approval, and if they don't get enough attention in positive ways, they'll find negative methods. They'll do things they know will be disapproved, because disapproval means attention.

Hurt and Attention

We often support and encourage the very behavior we would like to extinguish. We do this by paying attention to it, spending a lot of time admonishing the child for doing that particular thing. We find that giving attention reinforces specific behavior; that ignoring or not paying attention to undesirable behavior gradually extinguishes it.

Let me give some examples: when two young children are fighting, to whom do we usually pay the attention? We respond to the aggressor. "Can't you ever leave your brother alone? You're too big to be hitting him." The aggressor has successfully captured our attention, which is often why siblings fight in the first place.

We can handle it differently. When I see a child attack another, I say to the one who has been hit, "I'll bet you didn't like it when she hit you. Come and sit in my lap and I'll snuggle you. I'm sorry she hurt you." The one who did the hitting gets a clear message: there's no attention for her. She succeeded in catapulting her rival into the seat of honor. If she regularly gets this reaction to hitting, she will look for another way to get attention from adults.

If a young child falls and hurts herself, I do essentially the same thing. I ask the child to show me exactly where the hurt is. I put a hand carefully on that spot, and say "Tell me when to stop." Almost always, the word comes within ten seconds, and they are up and on their way.

We take children seriously. We give our full attention, and other children give them attention. We are letting them be in charge. They can have this attention for as long as they want it. As with so many things, once you get what you want, you don't need it any more. It is rare for a child to allow me to keep my hand on a hurt for more than a few seconds. If she does, I perk up my ears. I say to myself, "I want to pay extra attention to this child. This is someone who has been wanting more attention, and now that she has the opportunity, she's getting all she can." I may drop by with a few extra snuggles. Some have questioned this, surmising that such a technique will produce more hurts. In fact, I think it does the opposite. Children know that they will be taken seriously when necessary, so they don't have to manufacture situations to make us attend to them.

I find, as a teacher, that I am constantly having to make decisions. It feels sometimes like dozens in a minute. Later I may think it would have been better to have done things another way. I used to fault myself for this.

My husband told me that Babe Ruth was successful by hitting three or four times out of every ten. I don't miss on six or seven of ten decisions I make. From time to time I think about the Babe. I realize two things: I appreciate tremendously my husband's ability to reassure me with such subtlety, and after three or four appropriate decisions I'm in the big leagues.

Giving attention to young children can be wearisome work, and I truly want to do it right. Often I confer with another teacher about a decision. Having time to do this is a great luxury. Children often ask one of us if they can do something, and go to someone else if the response is negative. Because we are in close proximity, and keep in touch with each other, the children find a consistency in our responses, and this provides them, over the long run, a feeling of security.

It's usually harder for parents and caregivers, often the sole adult in attendance, to check in as we can at school. I think it is always all right for parents to postpone a decision, saying that they need to talk with the other parent, or with other adults who involve themselves with the children's lives. At school we often delay a decision, saying "I need to think about that for a minute," or "I'll talk to the other teacher." Then we put our heads together. I think it's just as well, in fact, for young children to note that adults help each other, confer, change their minds and attitudes when pertinent factors are brought up by another.

It is generally useful to step back from the position of being a parent; this may be done with the help of another person or by careful note-taking. Surprising insight may come from a careful look at the patterns of your household's behavior. When distressing incidents occur, what precedes them? It may be simpler than you imagine, involving the eating of certain foods or too little sleep. It may be more complicated. Think about all the relationships in the group, and the likes and dislikes among and between the members. Behavior is always caused by something.

I once heard a parent say to his child as he hit her, "This will teach you not to hit." I recognize with sorrow that his child will probably continue hitting.

When we offer help and attention to our children when it is genuinely needed, if our tones are friendly, if we look for aspects of our children that please us, and if we let our children know we appreciate them, they are likely to want to emulate us. Parents are gods to children. There is no one children want more to be like than their parents, if the relationship is strong and loving. When we act in ways we would like our children to act, we are well on the way to having the children we most want.

Praise and Expectations

Do we expect too much of our children? Too little? What do we communicate to them of our expectations? Do we say at one moment, "You're a big boy now; you shouldn't wet your pants," and turn around and say, "Oh, no, you're much too small to go to the concert with Daddy. Wait until you're older"? Does it sometimes seem to them that they are never the right size or age?

I know parents who expect so much of their children that the children always fail. They can't measure up to their parents' expectations. I also know parents who expect so little that their children remain babies; they talk baby talk, they whine, they are dependent, and they don't act as do others their age. Fortunately I also know parents who seem able to strike a balance, letting their children have the power to make their own decisions when they can, letting them know that their elders will make sure that they are safe, and will take care of them when appropriate.

We all live up to the expectations of those around us, or try to. If someone expects us to be competent, it calls upon all of our resources; we do our best in that situation. On the other hand, we may easily give up, or do things only passably well when people indicate that we probably aren't up to it. We thrive on other people's confidence in us, but it must bear some relationship to our capabilities. If someone indicates that she expects me to understand the nuclear physics on which she is about to expound, I feel inadequate and overwhelmed. I want the person with me to demonstrate some sensitivity to what I can do, and to what I can understand, and then to call on me to put all of myself into the task. I'm inspired, in other words, by the proper amount of confidence, and defeated by expectations which are too high.

How do you know how much to expect from your child? You can learn by careful observation; by reading about developmental stages and by talking with and observing other parents and other children. I see many parents sense when their child can be stretched a little, and when it is important to nurture them and accept them, without showing high expectations. When you figure out your child's capabilities in a given area, such as dressing, you can talk her through it, helping occasionally and showing no impatience. You can lay her pants on the floor and tell her that now she can stick her feet in the legs. You'll be standing by to make sure both legs don't go in one pant leg, and you can step in and help her straighten them out. You might not help physically at all, and offer only verbal assistance. "Yes, I can see that you know how to pull those pants up. You're doing it, even though it's a hard job. I remember when you couldn't do this at all. Now you're standing up and pulling your pants all the way up. Wow, you did it!" Words of encouragement, plus a little physical help, can do wonders for inspiring a child's confidence that she can do it herself.

Be flexible in these expectations. If a child is tired, or not feeling well, or upset, you need to lower your expectations. Your goal is for her to have many successes. If you don't vary your expectations with what you know of her present condition, you will set her up for failure. If she is tired and cranky, be assured that she will not be able to function as well as when she's in tip-top shape. Help her more in such situations. I can remember times when I completely dressed my four-year-old son, even though I knew he had done this many times himself. I remember feeling at those times that it was just too much for him. I didn't want him to fail, and I didn't want to find myself angry with him because of his failure. So I did it for him, lovingly, not grudgingly. I didn't say, "I don't know why you can't dress yourself today. You've done it every day for weeks and weeks." I also know that he appreciated my awareness of his differing needs. In no way did this set him back in his doing things for himself. In fact, it probably encouraged him, since he knew he wasn't going to be held accountable at every moment for everything he had ever learned up to that point.

Growth is not steady and even; it comes in spurts. It is as though the child coasts for a while and then surges suddenly ahead. New skills will be acquired at a great rate. Some will be forgotten and will have to be relearned. They will be practiced and practiced. Have you ever watched a child learning to tie her shoe (a complicated feat, indeed)? She works and works at this difficult task, trying to force her small muscles to go through very tricky work. She struggles with the coordination necessary. When she learns it, she does it over and over again. Sometimes, it still doesn't come out right. For a long time, not having learned the subtleties of pulling the knot exactly tight, she finds it coming quickly undone. Eventually, it stays tied for longer and longer. What an accomplishment! What a movement into the adult world she so strives to join.

It takes much more time to stand by and watch while she ties her shoes than it does for you to do it yourself. Supporting a child as she grows in independence is a time-consuming job. Unfortunately, much of parenting is rush, rush, rush. It's hard to take the time to let your child perform her newly acquired skills when you are hurrying to work and have to drop her off at preschool on the way. Perhaps it helps to think of yourself as an educator as well as a parent. Perhaps then you can be more aware of the importance of waiting that extra minute or three minutes for her to do something by herself. It's not easy.

One of the luxuries I have enjoyed as a preschool teacher, a luxury I rarely had as a parent, is the great gift of time. I had little else on my mind as a teacher. My schedule was geared to the pace of the children, and I had all the time necessary to be patient while they struggled through learning processes. I could support, help, advise, guide, and I could help them finish a task with a feeling of success. "I did it myself!" It's not easy to maintain this sort of patience as a parent or caretaker.

The pace is faster. There are more things that absolutely must be done. I know that a caretaker cannot take the time that a preschool teacher can; I plead, though, for awareness on the parent's part of the struggle for growth and accomplishment that goes on inside your child all of the time. When you see it clearly, you can sometimes slow the pace so that she can succeed.

Nobody wants to be told they're doing a poor job. None of us wants to be instructed on how to do something better than we're doing it. Who wants to feel that their character is being assassinated? And yet, how often do we talk this way to our children? We tell them, essentially, that they are stupid. We sometimes tell them they'll never learn to do it right.

Part of our job as raisers of children is to instruct them in the proper ways of doing things. We don't think of ourselves as teachers, but we are. Successful teachers give clear instructions and follow up by visibly noticing when and where their students succeed. They pay less attention to when and where they fail. I'm concerned that many of us, as parents, don't often teach in this fashion. We focus too often, I think, on our children's failings. It's failure that we think is staring us in the face. If Mathilda cleaned her room by stuffing everything under the bed, we forget to tell her that she managed to get her floor very clean. We focus on the cache under the bed. We could, if we thought about it, say something like, "Mathilda, I see that you got everything off of the middle of your floor! Now you'll be able to walk around your room without stepping on things! I see that you did it by sliding everything under your bed. Let's both get down here, and I'll hand you things so that you can put each one away. I'll bet it seemed like an awfully big job to do that by yourself." You hand her things, sorting as you go, so that she might get three things together that go in the same place. In short order the floor is cleared, and Mathilda is feeling supported and loved, instead of feeling criticized and a failure.

We may say, with truth, "But I don't have the time to do this with her." Or, "She should learn to do that by herself." We usually spend a lot of time and energy yelling at our children about how poorly they are doing something. We come back time after time, and they still haven't done the job. It often takes no more total time to lend a hand. She will learn to do the whole job herself after a few lessons by a supportive parent. A floor full of toys and clothing can be overwhelming to a young child. Teaching how to sort into categories can be an invaluable aid. And while we are teaching sorting, we can have a good time with the child. Let's not end with a statement like "I hope you remember this lesson and don't let it get this way again." It will be a huge mess again, and it'll be soon. Children can't look ahead to see in their mind's eye the mess they are making. They are creatures of the moment. They're focusing on what they are doing, not on the long-term consequences. We can be on the same side as our children, and not have to play the part of the adversary.

When we have helped them complete a task, such as cleaning their room, we can say, "We're really quite a team. We know how to work together. I was the sorter and you put the things away. Next time we might switch places, if you want. Would you like that?" We are helping them understand the process by describing how we worked. We're giving them a voice in the process by offering to switch roles. Children need adults to describe processes. They are so centered in the moment that they often don't see the whole. The parent might have said, during the clean-up time, "Do you want to put clothes away first, or toys first?" Such words help the child see the sorting process as a whole.

At no time during this episode does the parent tell the child, "You are a bad girl," or "You are such a good girl." It never makes sense to make a judgment about the character of a child. It is appropriate to describe what the child is doing. One might say, "You've learned to sort your toys so quickly," or "It's still very hard for you to sort your toys. It's a big job. Let me help you. Shall we do the big ones first or the little ones?" Each of these statements describes a process, and offers a certain amount of choice. They do not evaluate the child or her worth. Descriptions like this teach, and evaluative words don't. Rewards and punishments don't usually move a child along her path to growth and learning.

Egocentricity

Young children think they are the center of the universe. In general, they think they are responsible for things that happen around them such as death, divorce and other catastrophes. It is not surprising that they develop this attitude. From their first days, if they were well cared for, someone came when they cried. Someone fed them when they were hungry. When they were wet, they were changed; when they smiled, someone smiled back. In fact, they were the center of their parents' universe.

This attitude can lead to all sorts of confusion. They are just beginning to be able to see things from another's point of view. It's generally pointless to say to a young child "Can't you see that she doesn't like it when you do that?" They look at the world, for the most part, from their eyes only. They have little sense that others might hurt as they do. You can say "He doesn't like it," or "I don't like it when you do that." Even if they don't understand it, they gradually come to know this is true.

From this point of egocentricity, young children are sure they are responsible for their parents' divorce, for their grandmother's death, and for other family catastrophes. I think it is a rare child of divorced parents who feels her parents would not have divorced had she been a better child. Although she was probably given some information about the reason for the divorce, she still is likely to believe, deep inside, that she could have prevented it had she somehow been different, better, smarter. To this day I entertain doubts amid embarrassment about my own parents' divorce.

Death is another very large hurdle for young children to surmount. Most young children experience moments of wishing that someone in their family would die, or disappear, or radically change. If that person actually dies, young children may well feel they have caused it. As food arrives when they are hungry, so does death come when beckoned. Young children experience a state of magic; they think they have special powers. Power is particularly confusing because young children occasionally feel that they have extraordinary power, even though they more often feel they have very little power. I once read an account of an incident that saddens me. A child, her mother and grandmother were shopping in a store. The child bumped into the grandmother, who fell over and died! You can imagine the strong sense of magic powers that child may have felt. I would assume that the child was consumed with guilt. There before her, in a more direct way than is usually true, was the evidence that she had caused her grandmother's death. It is important to remember the depth of such a sense of causality, and to reassure children, when hard things occur, that they are not responsible. One might say, "We are very sad that grandmother died. I will certainly miss her! I remember what good times we had with her, when she told you stories and we went on trips with her. And it was not your fault that she died. It was time for her to die. You did not make her die."

When one considers this aspect of egocentricity, of being the center of the world, it is easier to understand why it is hard for young children to share their possessions. Think of the difficulty young children feel when their parents are about to have another child, and they're faced with the prospect of sharing their parents! Understanding this can help us be more tolerant of their behavior and of their fears. Their behavior is not perverse; it is logical, and it is as if they speak a different language. You may use the same words they do, but they may have utterly different meanings. I remember sitting with a friend who had a four-year-old son, who was playing nearby. We thought he was absorbed in his play and oblivious of us. One of us said, "My, he is small for his age." He reacted with immediate disgust. I then said, "He has sharp ears." He slowly, carefully felt all around each of his ears. "I do *not* have sharp ears!" he cried. Young children sometimes misunderstand a great deal of the conversation that swirls about them, although the feelings inherent in the words often come through very strongly, if skewed. Their frame of reference is different; their understanding of words is often limited. Much of what they hear may be frightening. Although they feel powerful (in that they see themselves as the cause of much of what happens around them), it is an uncomfortable form of power, and at the same time they are aware that they often have little say in the determination of their lives. We tell children to eat, dress, bathe, get ready for school, go to sleep. It appears to them that our whims are their lot. The world is made for adults. Chairs, tables and kitchen counters are all too high for them. Most people tower over them. I remember seeing some photographs shot by a photographer who wanted to make this point. He lay on the floor and photographed from the vantage point of a young child. He saw the undersides of tables. People were huge. Their nostrils and eyes bore down on him. I sometimes lie down on the floor to experience briefly this sense of size.

It is very helpful to put ourselves in the shoes of our children from time to time. Motivations make more sense when we stop to consider their source. We usually find that what strikes us as annoying or perverse is something else altogether. Children may hold an entirely different notion in their minds than do we, though our conversation belies it. When we find ourselves struggling over time or issues of power with children, we might try to step back and see what is really going on. Is it a power struggle? Or is this child on a different wave length? It's hard to take the time and the care to reflect upon such questions, but often highly productive when we can do it.

It is equally important to allow our children to make mistakes. In our wisdom we want to save them from mistakes. Haven't we learned a tremendous amount from mistakes, though? We tried something; it didn't work. We look around for other solutions, and we develop our creativity, our patience, our delight in exploration. When we have the confidence to err, we are less likely to make disastrous mistakes.

We can let our children know that we have confidence in their ability to solve problems. With constant orders and instructions, one can gain little practice in decision-making. Young people have no reason to carry self-confidence if they have little opportunity to take risks. Think of the kind of adults we want our children to be. We want them to be both strong and empathetic.

Sharing

HELPING TO FIND SOLUTIONS

For many parents of young children, sharing is high on the list of goals for their children. I personally consider the word 'sharing' an unhelpful word when speaking of and to young children. I think it means this to them: "I can't have what I want. I have to give it away." This makes sense, when we think about it. When we tell them to share, we are really asking them to give something to somebody else.

The concept of sharing, however, is extremely useful. A child often will suddenly want a toy when she thinks another child is about to take it. We all have a little of this greed within us. If two children fight over a toy, I urge them to talk it over and settle it themselves. This takes lots of practice on their part. At the beginning of their learning to do this, I might say, "I see two children and one toy dog. I wonder what we can do about this." Then I sit near and watch their faces. I repeat what each has to say. Out of their words often come the descriptive facts. "I had it first," "But I want it." When the problem is as clear as this, the question "When you are through with it, will you give it to Henry?" might solve the problem, because, although I am solving it for them, I am giving the decision-making power to the child. All children not only want power, they need it.

When it is not so simple, I stay with them, repeating their words. From time to time I may say, "I wonder how you can work this out? Any ideas?" Often one will say, "I know. I'll have it first, and then give it to Zoe." This may or may not be acceptable to Zoe. I stay nearby, trying hard not to offer solutions, to keep them at the process of problem-solving. I believe that this process is what's important, not the solution. The more experience children have with this process, the more capable they are of finding their own solutions. Often a child finds an acceptable substitute toy for the other child. Sometimes one realizes that she is not that interested in getting the toy, particularly after seeing that her want is taken seriously even though her instant attainment is not guaranteed.

The more adults help children find solutions, the more we are helping them develop lifelong tools. We often operate on the assumption that solving things quickly is paramount. I think it's worth a great deal of time and energy if we can enable them to do this for themselves. Negotiating skills are used effectively by many adults, but many others have never grasped them very well.

In negotiating situations, as in so many others, we want to transfer the power to the child. We want to phase ourselves out and let young people take charge. As always, we try to take the long view.

When a child is asked to give a toy to another when she is finished with it, the power is put in her hands. Initially, she may say, "I'm never going to be through with it! I'm going to use it all day long!" As she gets used to her power, she frequently uses it magnanimously, giving the toy to the other. Children's attention span is often short, and unless the power struggle holds their interest, they're not so deeply committed to keeping control of the toy anyway. In our preschool, I frequently hear children calling out, "I'm done with this now; you can have it!" I enjoy hearing it.

FRUSTRATION LESSONS

Most children are largely self-centered in their early years. Each child knows that on many levels she is the center of the universe, even when she is neglected or abused. An empathetic, pleasant child may feel deeply for others at times, but still see herself as the middle of everything. When she cries, people react to her, whether nurturing or in anger. When she wants things she usually gets them. When a child meets up with other self-centered beings, struggles ensue. Each child thinks she can have anything, everything, at any time.

Emily is building with blocks. So is her friend Jasper. He has a block that she wants. Emily grabs it; Jasper hits her. Emily cries. An adult comes and says, "Why can't you play nicely? Jasper, why can't you give her that block; you have lots more?"

What is the adult teaching both children? Emily learns that she can have what she wants if she makes enough noise, and that grabbing is really all right. Jasper learns that life is not fair. An adult sides against him, and he may have to be sneaky to get back at Emily. He may also believe that boys are often blamed when they struggle with girls.

Parents can help their children to get along in life by giving them frustration lessons. Parents can find situations where they can stop giving in to their children. When a parent joins a child in block play, the parent can be unwilling to give up any block the child demands. The parent can say, "I'm using this now. I'll give it to you when I'm through with it." This method can help the child to learn to wait for a turn, and to delay having all her wishes fulfilled. It's the core of civilization, learning that one can't have what one wants when one wants it. A child can sometimes more easily accept frustration lessons from a parent or teacher than from a young playmate who might be unfriendly to the idea.

A parent who read this said, "This is in direct contradiction to your ideas about letting children take the lead in playing with adults, and also with your conviction that we should try to say 'yes' to children whenever possible." It's an astute observation, and yet I disagree with the result of her conclusion. Saying yes and relinquishing the lead are different than letting a child take a toy from your hand, or demanding immediate gratification. The father (elsewhere in the book) who plays with his child in the sandbox, following the child's lead, would still be reluctant to give up his stick or pail if his child demanded it. In fact, we say 'yes' in a deeper sense to young children by treating them fairly and expecting them to treat us fairly.

When children have been on center stage for a long time, both as a natural result of the way children view the world and as a consequence of adults giving in to them easily, it takes a long time to gradually learn to shift attitudes. We need to have patience, and we need to model this behavior. Above all we need to realize that frustration is a natural consequence of life, and that learning to deal with it is useful and healthy.

Problem-Solving

Problems are always with us. We need skills in problem-solving, but how often are we taught them? We can offer our young children this training on a daily basis. A child says, "How do you open this box?" We can respond, "Mm, I wonder . . . How do you suppose you do it?" We are showing interest in the problem, and supporting the child in striving for a solution. We need to stay nearby, continuing to give encouraging words. "You're really working on this problem! You're trying lots of different ways." Children who are encouraged will work for a long time solving problems. At times they may need more than words. Perhaps a hand pushing or pulling along with theirs will be welcome, as long as the helper is working with them, not doing it for them. If, after a long struggle, a stronger, bigger person steps in and does it for a child, her sense of power may be wiped out. If the task is truly too hard for the child to do alone, we pitch in, giving more help as we talk the child through the task, "Look, we did it together!" She'll realize it was a cooperative endeavor. One of our main tasks in raising children is to encourage them to try, to figure out, to struggle, to persist. The successful outcome of such persistent attention gives the child a bonus: a feeling of power.

Young children find it tricky to put on snow pants, so they often resist wearing them. I have taught many children to put on this hated piece of clothing. I lay the snow pants on the floor with straps tucked out of the way. I guide the child to the proper end of the pants. I sit her down, barely starting the first foot into a leg. From then I mostly watch and cheer her on, "Yes, you're pulling up that leg . . . Now pull a little on the other. Look, one foot is nearly through; I can see your toes peeking out." A pep talk like this lets the child know that it is possible, and that you won't leave her adrift. She can see that she's making progress. At times I may give a little pull on the pants, or on her leg. The child does most of the work, so she feels a real sense of accomplishment when the job is done.

Another major problem for children is jackets. Lay the jacket on the floor with its arms spread out and the front of the jacket exposed. Ask the child to stand at the top of the jacket. (This seems so strange that it is often hard for them to do this. You can laugh together about the humor in the situation.) They then reach down, slide their arms in the sleeves, toss the jacket over their heads, and presto! The jacket is on.

So much of the time young people feel so powerless that it is no wonder that they develop periods of negativity. They are resisting the power they feel all around them. In fact, if a child did not resist some of the time, we would eventually fault her for being too compliant. Remember that it seems to them that everyone else knows more than they do. Getting a handle on the solving of problems, and building up practice in carrying it out, will bring confidence in its wake.

Decision-Making

Making decisions is often even harder for children than it is for adults. Many of us didn't get much practice dealing with choices when we were young. Our parents decided everything for us. If that was so, it's no wonder that we have trouble in this area as grown-ups. How can we prevent our children from coming up against this same difficulty?

Children constantly face situations in which they can make choices. It's important for us as parents and teachers to help children become aware of these opportunities. "Which shoe are you going to put on first? Do you want a banana or an apple? What shape blocks are you going to put away first?" Young children are making choices all the time. We can help them realize that they are choosing. We might say, "I can see that you thought a lot before you chose this apple. Sometimes it's hard to make decisions. Sometimes we want both things."

We can give children more voice in family decisions. We can include them in planning menus, plotting family road trips, decorating their own room or other places in the apartment or house. Children need lots of practice making decisions, and they need to know they are doing so. I have seen children paralyzed when the time came to make a decision, unable to choose between going to the housekeeping area in school, or the blocks, or the paints. A child looks around helplessly. What is she using as the basis for her decision? Is it the other people already in each spot, or her own preference? We often take a child by the hand and walk around, talking about what is going on in each area, helping her focus on the specifics. I consider this to be training in decision-making.

Sometimes there are too many choices. Some children need the situation simplified. Two things from which to choose are often easier than many. Children can graduate to more complicated decision-making as they run into opportunities to practice it.

We are models for our children. They observe us, and assimilate a great deal of what they see us do and say. When we make decisions clearly and simply, they notice this. We can talk about our own difficulties and triumphs in decision-making. We can model for them by usually sticking to decisions, and not grieving if later evidence indicates a poor decision. Perhaps we're afraid that because of their inexperience they will make mistakes. Let's help them see that mistakes are an integral part of making decisions, and that mistakes are all right. If we accept errors and mistakes with equanimity, young people are likely to make better choices later in life, when bigger consequences usually follow. We can comfort them when their decisions turn out unsatisfactorily and affirm them when they make decisions they feel good about. We can remark, "It looks as though you are really learning how to make decisions. You have an easier time deciding, and later you are usually happy with what you chose." Affirm, affirm, affirm; we can't do enough of it. We're helping our children feel good about themselves and about the processes they employ to make choices and decisions, something that will give them self-confidence throughout their lives.

About the Author

Barbara Hill was born in Boston in 1920. She went to schools in New York City, Fairhope, Alabama, and Laguna Beach, California. She graduated from Black Mountain College, a small, very progressive liberal arts college in North Carolina. She met and married Mort Steinau at Black Mountain, and they have three children.

Her father was a teacher and summer camp director, her mother a social worker. From them she learned to be an independent and clear thinker, to be aware of people around her, their differences and needs, and to act on her beliefs whether popular or not. She has been a peace activist and worker for racial equality for many decades. Since retiring to Cape Cod in 1990, she has continued to speak out, to write, and to organize non-violent vigils against U.S. military excursions and to teach workshops and classes on racism.

It is from this background that her teaching developed: her innovative, unconventional view of teaching, assisting children to learn rather than to "teach" them. And it is, in turn, from this background that the book speaks: to teachers who've never been in her classroom, and to parents, guardians and caregivers, enabling them to assist children in becoming as creative, effective, self-esteeming, caring, life-enjoying as it's possible for each of them to be.

An educator for fifty years, Barbara Hill Steinau was founder, director and teacher of preschools in Connecticut and is currently a preschool consultant and activist on Cape Cod. She founded a cooperative nursery in Killingworth, Connnecticut and opened a preschool at the Connnecticut Hospice in Branford, which she ran for ten years. This was a school for healthy children from nearby towns, in a wing of the hospice. The location was specific, to remind staff, patients and patients' families that life does go on.

Throughout her years of teaching, she found teaching teachers and parents as important to her as working with young children. She says, "Teachers I've trained have also been my teachers." In this book she continues that work. To honor her, and to carry on her work and philosophy, teachers and parents founded the Steinau School for Young Children in Hamden, Connecticut.

Barabara Hill Steinau has previously published in *Young Children*, the journal of the National Association of Young Children. Should you wish to share thoughts about this book with her, you can e-mail her at: barbmort@capecod.net.